I0815972

MY NEW INDIAN KITCHEN

MY NEW INDIAN KITCHEN

VIKRAM VIJ

WITH JENNIFER MUTTOO

Vancouver/Toronto/Berkeley

This is to all my guests who have made
Vij's Restaurant what it is today!

To my partner, who helps me believe
that the most important thing in life is to
enjoy every moment. You have motivated me
and shown me that anything is possible.

To my daughters, Nanaki and Shanik,
thank you for reminding me to dream big.

Live life on your own terms and let creativity flow without boundaries. Be free and do whatever the F**K you want. —Vikram Vij

CONTENTS

COOK WITH YOUR HEART, EAT WITH YOUR HANDS

The word for "freedom" in Hindi is स्वतंत्रता (*swatantrata*). It signifies the state of being free and independent, or having the liberty to act, speak or think without undue restraint. It encompasses both personal and political freedoms.

Life's journey can sometimes lead us down unexpected paths, filled with twists and turns that test our resilience and spirit. For me, the culinary world has been both a refuge and a lifelong passion, especially during times of personal challenge and heartache.

Losing love and struggling through a failing marriage brought me to a profound low point, where I questioned life's blessings and uncertainties. Yet, amid this turmoil, I found solace in the unwavering love I have for food and the art of cooking—the light at the end. The food and beverage industry is no stranger to fractured relationships, but I discovered that my kitchen was a steadfast companion throughout these trials.

Growing up in a culture where arranged marriages are common, I experienced firsthand that while this tradition works for many, it was not my path to love. Instead, I rediscovered my true calling, my first love, within the bustling atmosphere of the kitchen—the heartbeat of my existence. The frenetic energy of this fast-paced environment, with its clattering plates and lively chaos, became my sanctuary—a place where passion and purpose converged. Here, amidst the hustle and bustle, I found peace and fulfillment.

Then, unexpectedly, outside the noise and heat of the kitchen, I met Jennifer, who mirrored the harmony and contentment I felt within my culinary domain. Our meeting sparked an instant emotional connection. Our conversations flowed effortlessly and were driven by our shared knowledge of—and passion for—the food, beverage and hospitality industry.

This pivotal moment marked the convergence of my personal and professional journeys—a testament to the precious bonds that form in the deepest connections. Since then, we've worked on countless collaborations, almost always centered around our love for creating memorable culinary experiences. Jennifer, who I call Jaan, was instrumental in the making of this cookbook, along with many changes that have occurred at Vij's Restaurant.

LETCHMI VILAS
N AR NACHIAPPA CHETTIAR
A MUTHUPATNAM
PARKING

Cook with your heart… When I was young, I loved experimenting with spices and cooking, even with something as simple as rice pudding. I enjoyed adding new ingredients to create something different and unique. That same philosophy is present today at Vij's. We don't follow a recipe book or strict standards—our cooks have the freedom to make food that's tasty and well-prepared, cooking with love and passion. People should embrace our food for what it is, at face value, without making comparisons to other chefs or restaurants. I feel the same applies when making food at home: I want my readers to cook for fulfilment, for growth, for you. For that reason, whenever you see this icon, I have included my tips on cooking with passion, love and a personal touch.

Eat with your hands… When we first created our lamb popsicles, I named them that because so many people were using knives and forks to eat our lamb. I wanted to encourage them to pick up the bones and eat with their hands, as I believe it makes the food taste better. I joke that after eating my food, they should run their hands through their hair so it will become curly like mine—of course, it's all in good fun! People often take me seriously, though. In South India, licking your fingers after a meal is considered the highest form of compliment. I always tell people, "You don't make love with a knife or fork, so why eat with one?"

Eating with your hands connects you to the food in a way that utensils simply can't. It allows you to fully engage with the textures, temperatures and flavors of the meal, making the experience more personal and intimate. It's also a way to show respect for the chef, as it reflects a deeper appreciation for the craftsmanship and love that went into preparing the dish. In this book, I've included tips marked with this icon to encourage you to break free from formality, embrace the joy of eating with your hands and engage more deeply with your meal. It's a reminder to enjoy the simple, primal act of eating, letting go of the constraints of dining etiquette to connect more fully with your food.

I'VE COME TO REALIZE the things that matter most to me and I celebrate them with you in this cookbook. Here, I invite you into my culinary world—a world where love, resilience and the joy of cooking intertwine to create dishes that nourish both the body and the soul. Each recipe is infused with a piece of my story, a tale of finding love and purpose amid life's challenges, one dish at a time. Join me on this culinary adventure, and may these recipes inspire you as they have inspired me.

Dietary Symbols

This book includes symbols for common dietary needs, making it easier for readers to identify dishes that fit their preferences or restrictions. Whether you're looking for vegetarian, gluten-free or other options, these symbols ensure a more personalized cooking experience.

VEGETARIAN	Vegetarian
VEGAN	Vegan
GF	Gluten-free
NF	Nut-free
DF	Dairy-free
<5	Five ingredients or fewer

Recipe Notes

Unless otherwise stated:

Milk is whole.

Rice is basmati.

Flour is all-purpose.

Eggs are large.

Pepper is freshly ground.

Produce is medium.

Sugar is granulated/white.

RESTAURANT, HISTORY AND CULTURAL SIGNIFICANCE

Vij's underwent a remarkable transformation during the challenges of Covid-19, merging functionality with artistry. Adorned with decorative yellow terrazzo flowers, the lounge tabletops designed by Marc Bricault not only added beauty but also provided a safe dining space when needed.

The standout paisley bar table, ingeniously crafted from old beer and wine bottles from Vij's by Marc and Walter Gibson, is a tribute to its glory days as a cherished spot at the former Vij's in South Granville, where figures such as Harrison Ford, Martha Stewart and Robin Williams gathered at one time or another over the years.

The pomegranate flower artwork, also created by Marc and Walter, holds profound cultural meaning. In Indian tradition, the pomegranate symbolizes fertility and life—a representation of the essence of women. This artwork is a powerful expression of life's abundance.

Inspired by the vibrant red walls of Rangoli, the former sister restaurant in South Granville, the terrazzo tables in the Vij's lounge evoke a lively appetite (it has been proven that the color red whets the appetite). They symbolize a new beginning, blending seamlessly with the restaurant's vibrant atmosphere.

I designed our kitchen to follow a classic French layout, with appetizers prepared on the left and main courses on the right, with a show kitchen for final plating and garnishing.

Within the kitchen's walk-in area, labels in Punjabi adorn cooked foods and spices, honoring the dedicated kitchen staff who have traveled from India to Canada in pursuit of a better life and a shared culinary vision.

Giving Back: Supporting the Downtown Eastside Women's Centre

Supporting women—especially those facing challenging situations with children—has always been a cause close to my heart. The Downtown Eastside Women's Centre (DEWC) in Vancouver provides a critical lifeline, offering safety, support and hope to those in need. Every year, I bring a hot, home-cooked meal to the shelter on Christmas Day, ensuring that these women and children can gather around a table, share a comforting meal and feel cared for during a time that can otherwise be incredibly difficult.

At Vij's Restaurant, we are proud to financially support this incredible cause each year, helping the shelter continue its vital work. The DEWC relies on the generosity of our community, and anyone can make a difference. To give back, contact engagement@dewc.ca to learn how you can support the DEWC. Together, we can create safety, warmth and hope for those who need it most.

Supporting all individuals within our community is essential to fostering a society where everyone has the opportunity to thrive, no matter their circumstances. By coming together, we can create a stronger, more compassionate world where no one is left behind.

FOOD FOR CHANGE

Food has always been at the heart of my life, not only as a source of nourishment but as a way to connect with others, especially those in need. Growing up in India, I witnessed the harsh realities of poverty, which deepened my desire to give back. Partnering with Cooks Who Feed has provided a meaningful way to make that difference.

Through this initiative, we've embraced a simple yet powerful model: 1 apron = 100 meals.

For every apron sold, 100 nutritious meals are provided to those facing hunger. This remarkable achievement demonstrates the power of small actions—by simply purchasing an apron, individuals are directly contributing to the fight against hunger and making a tangible difference within their communities.

And our efforts wouldn't be possible without the support of trusted organizations like No Kid Hungry and Rescuing Leftover Cuisine in the US, and Second Harvest in Canada. These partners have a proven track record of delivering food to those who need it most, ensuring that our efforts are truly impactful.

More than a third of our profits are directed to these charity partners, helping us fulfill our promise and inspire a ripple effect of positive change. Together, we can make a lasting difference, one meal at a time.

RAISE A GLASS

When I first opened Vij's, there was a misconception about Indian food—that it was cheap, overly spicy and best paired with inexpensive beer. It became my mission to challenge that idea by not only presenting our dishes with love and attention to detail, but also by pairing them with exceptional drinks that elevated the dining experience. We introduced a carefully crafted cocktail menu and began pairing our curries with local BC wines, which was a bold move at the time. The response was incredible, and it showed that the right drink—whether wine or a thoughtfully designed cocktail—could truly enhance the flavors of Indian food. So, I'd like to *raise a glass* to the winemakers, winegrowers and farmers who produce the delicious fruits from one of the best farming regions in the world. NAMASTE to all of them.

VEGETARIAN

SERVES 2

Knowing ginger's natural digestive benefits and lemon's health-boosting properties, I created this invigorating non-alcoholic drink as a twist on classic lemonade. Perfectly refreshing, it's a favorite at Vij's on warm summer nights, and I love sweetening it with local honey to enhance its vibrant, zesty flavor.

Ginger Lemonade

Juice of 2–3 lemons
Sugar or honey, to taste
Pinch of salt
1 tsp grated ginger
Mint leaves, for garnish (optional)

1 Combine all ingredients, except mint, in a large pitcher. Add 4 cups of water and stir until sugar has dissolved.

2 Garnish with mint (if using) and serve chilled.

GF NF DF VEGAN

SERVES 2

When I was a young boy playing outdoors in the heat of India, my mother would make me this restorative Indian mocktail to cool down and keep my energy up. With its bold herbal and spiced flavors, it's an acquired taste, but the perfect elixir when you need a feel-good energy boost—much like the effect of the electrolytes found in sports drinks in North America.

Jaljeera

2 Tbsp cumin seeds
1 Tbsp mango powder (*amchur*)
1 tsp black salt (see ♥)
½ tsp pepper
½ tsp ground ginger
¼ tsp ground cloves
Mint leaves, for garnish

♥ Black salt, or *kala namak*, is a mineral-rich salt with a distinct smoky, tangy flavor that is a cornerstone of Indian cuisine. Its unique taste enhances the complexity of dishes, from street food like *chaat* to refreshing beverages like *pani puri* and *lassi*. It can be found at specialty South Asian grocery stores.

1. Toast cumin seeds in a frying pan over medium heat until aromatic. Set aside to cool. Using a mortar and pestle, grind into a fine powder.
2. In a large pitcher, combine ground cumin and the remaining spices.
3. Add 4 cups of water to the spice mixture and stir well until combined.
4. Add ice, garnish with mint and serve chilled.

<5 GF NF DF VEGAN

SERVES 2

I have a deep love for gardening, and roses are grown both at my home and at Vij's. In fact, tourists from all over the world flock to Vancouver just to admire the stunning roses in Stanley Park. Inspired by this beauty, this drink is like presenting your guests with a bouquet of roses, filled with beautiful floral aromas.

Rose Sherbet

1 cup sugar

½ cup fresh or dried organic rose petals, plus extra for garnish

1–2 Tbsp lemon juice

A few drops of rose essence (see ♥)

♥ Rose essence brings a lovely floral touch to mixed drinks, adding a hint of elegance and depth. You can easily find it at specialty stores or online to elevate your cocktail game.

1. In a saucepan, combine sugar and 1 cup of water. Bring to a boil and stir until sugar dissolves.
2. Add rose petals and simmer for 3 minutes. Set aside to cool, then strain out rose petals.
3. Stir in lemon juice and rose essence.
4. In a blender, combine with ice and blend until smooth, or serve chilled over ice. Garnish with rose petals.

VEGETARIAN

SERVES 2

Lassi is a refreshing and creamy yogurt drink that captures the essence of Indian street food culture. Traditionally served in disposable clay cups, it's a beloved treat enjoyed by many. While Mango Lassi (page 33) is the most popular flavor in India, I love using berries to create a delicious twist on this classic. For a lighter option, you can also make it with buttermilk.

Berry Lassi

1 cup plain yogurt or buttermilk
½ cup blueberries or raspberries
2 Tbsp sugar, plus extra to taste
Pinch of ground cardamom (optional)

1. In a blender, combine yogurt (or buttermilk), berries, sugar and ½ cup of water. Blend until smooth.
2. Add ice, if desired, and blend again.
3. Pour into glasses, then sprinkle with cardamom (if using).
4. Enjoy immediately!

MOBILES
SALES
& SERVICE

VEGETARIAN

SERVES 1

This traditional Indian roadside drink is enjoyed by many Indians when we want to cool down on warm days. The mango can be replaced with any fruit, but the rich, creamy texture combined with the natural sweetness of the mango makes this version especially indulgent.

Mango Lassi

1 cup plain yogurt
1 ripe mango, diced
½ cup milk
2–3 Tbsp sugar, to taste
Pinch of ground cardamom (optional)

1. Combine all ingredients in a blender and blend until smooth and creamy.
2. Pour into a glass with ice, if desired, and serve chilled.

VEGETARIAN

SERVES 1–2

Every region in India has its own style of making chai, each with its own unique blend of spices and preparation method. Chai is not just a drink; it's an integral part of Indian culture, symbolizing warmth, hospitality and connection. I've been serving my version at Vij's for thirty years, and I personally deliver them to guests when they must stand in long lineups on cold nights, offering a comforting moment in the midst of the wait.

Masala Chai

2–3 green cardamom pods, slightly crushed

2–3 cloves

1 small cinnamon stick

1 small slice ginger, crushed

1 Tbsp black tea leaves

½ cup milk

Sugar, to taste

1. Bring 1 cup of water to a boil in a small saucepan. Add cardamom, cloves, cinnamon and ginger and boil for a few minutes to release the flavors.
2. Add tea leaves and boil for another 2 minutes.
3. Pour in milk and stir in sugar. Bring to a gentle boil.
4. Strain chai into cups and serve hot.

SPICE AND SOUL

Masala chai, meaning "spiced tea" in Hindi, is a delightful blend of Indian flavors—a brew of black tea with aromatic spices, sugar and milk. This iconic drink is deeply rooted in India's rich tea history, where resourceful workers used left-over tea leaves to create a flavorful chai. I truly believe that chai brings people together, fostering warm conversations and shared moments.

In addition to chai's rich history, Indian chai cups, known in Hindi as *kulhad chai*, hold special significance. These handleless earthenware cups connect us to an ancient Indian culture, allowing tea lovers to experience chai in a completely unique and authentic way. Furthermore, the handmade clay cups contribute to reducing plastic pollution, offering an eco-friendly alternative for the cherished tradition.

As a tribute to this meaningful custom, the ceilings of the restaurant's lounge are adorned with these cups, symbolizing their deep personal significance to me. We also serve chai when patrons need to wait in long lineups for a table and after their meal, as a gesture of traditional Indian warmth. This timeless beverage, a staple at social gatherings, embodies two of the most important mainstays of our restaurant: hospitality and conversation.

<5 GF NF DF VEGETARIAN

SERVES 1

The title of this Indian Manhattan is a derivation of two words: Kuchh Nai is a blended whisky that is made in the style of Johnny Walker Black, which is beloved by Indians, who regard it as a prestigious whisky. *Jaan* means "my love" in Hindi, and Jaan is what I call my love.

Kuchh nai also means "nothing, my love" in Hindi. When a guest visits your home, you ask them what they would like to drink. Most people reply *kuchh nai*, which is the polite (yet contrary) way of expressing you'd like something to drink.

Kuchh Nai Jaan (Nothing, My Love)

Honey syrup

2 Tbsp honey

Cocktail

2 oz Kuchh Nai or Johnnie Walker Black whisky

2 tsp Honey Syrup (see here)

1 clove

2 cinnamon sticks (divided)

Honey syrup

1 Combine honey and 1 tablespoon of water in a small bowl or glass and mix well.

Cocktail

2 Add ice to an old-fashioned glass.

3 Combine whisky, honey syrup, clove and 1 cinnamon stick in a mixing glass. Add ice. Stir for 30 seconds, or just enough to cool the drink and dilute it a bit. Do not over-stir.

4 Strain the cocktail into the prepared glass. Grate a little bit of the remaining cinnamon stick on top to garnish, then serve.

<5 GF NF DF VEGAN

SERVES 1

This cocktail amuses me. It's inspired by the song "Anything You Can Do" by Betty Hutton and Vij's Rangoli Cucumber-Mint Vodka, which is an unusual yet great alternative to gin or scotch. It's a refreshing cucumber-mint beverage perfect for enjoying on a patio during a summer evening.

Anything You Can Do

- 1¾ oz vodka (preferably Vij's Rangoli Cucumber-Mint Vodka)
- ¼ oz St-Germain Elderflower Liqueur
- 1 oz soda water
- Dash of lime juice
- 1 lime wedge, for garnish

1. Add ice to a highball glass.
2. Add vodka and elderflower liqueur. Top with soda water and lime juice.
3. Garnish with lime wedge and serve with a compostable straw, if desired.

<5 GF NF DF VEGAN

SERVES 1

The British Raj is a gentle reminder of the colonial era when the British were reluctant to drink Indian water. Instead, they concocted a drink made with quinine, a traditional cure for malaria, and called it tonic water—then used it as a preventive measure against the disease, which was prevalent at the time. Unfortunately, it was too bitter to drink on its own, so British army officers combined it with lime, sugar, water and gin to make it more palatable. And that's how the classic gin and tonic (G&T) was born.

Our version is made with our own gin and garnished with mint, cucumber and a sliver of ginger. Prince Harry and Meghan Markle loved this drink when they dined at the restaurant.

British Raj (Vij's G&T)

2 oz gin (preferably Vij's Lantern Gin)
3 oz premium tonic water (preferably Fever-Tree)
Cucumber slice, for garnish
Sliver of ginger, for garnish
Large mint leaf, for garnish

1 Fill an old-fashioned glass with ice. Add gin and tonic and stir gently to mix.

2 With a cocktail pick, skewer cucumber, ginger and mint leaf. Place on top of the drink, then serve.

VEGETARIAN

SERVES 1

For this cocktail, homemade chai is prepared in-house with cardamom and combined with a shot of single malt whisky. Many cultures, such as Italian, have a tradition of serving a digestif, and this is my creation for Vij's.

Nice Guy Chai

- 1 oz single malt whisky (preferably Vij's Guru Sandalwood Finished Single Malt Whisky)
- 1 cup Masala Chai (page 35)

1. Combine whisky and masala chai in a mug and serve hot.

<5 GF NF DF VEGETARIAN

SERVES 1

Jennifer orders the same drink everywhere she goes for dinner—a whisky sour. While she is very adventurous in sampling different styles of cocktails, it is her go-to drink. Therefore, this delicious cocktail is included in her honor.

Jennifer's Whisky Sour

2 oz single malt whisky (preferably Vij's Guru Sandalwood Finished Single Malt Whisky)

1 oz lemon juice

½ oz rich simple syrup

Dash of bitters (preferably Fee Brothers Cardamom Bitters)

1 egg white or 2 Tbsp aquafaba (optional)

1. Fill a coupe glass with ice, if desired.
2. Add all ingredients to a cocktail shaker. If using egg white or aquafaba, seal the shaker and shake for 5 seconds to emulsify. (Keep a hand on both parts of the shaker to ensure it stays closed.) Unseal the shaker.
3. Add ice to the shaker. Seal and shake vigorously for 20 seconds.
4. Double strain into the prepared glass.

SERVES 1

Sometimes, the only satisfaction after a long day is a strong drink with tequila.

Satisfaction

1½ oz tequila or mezcal
1½ oz orange juice
½ oz Maraschino liqueur
1 oz pomegranate juice
Lager beer, to serve

1. Add ice to an old-fashioned glass.
2. Add ice to a shaker. Add all ingredients, except lager. Seal and shake vigorously for 20 seconds.
3. Double strain into the prepared glass.
4. Serve with a glass of lager on the side, taking turns sipping each.

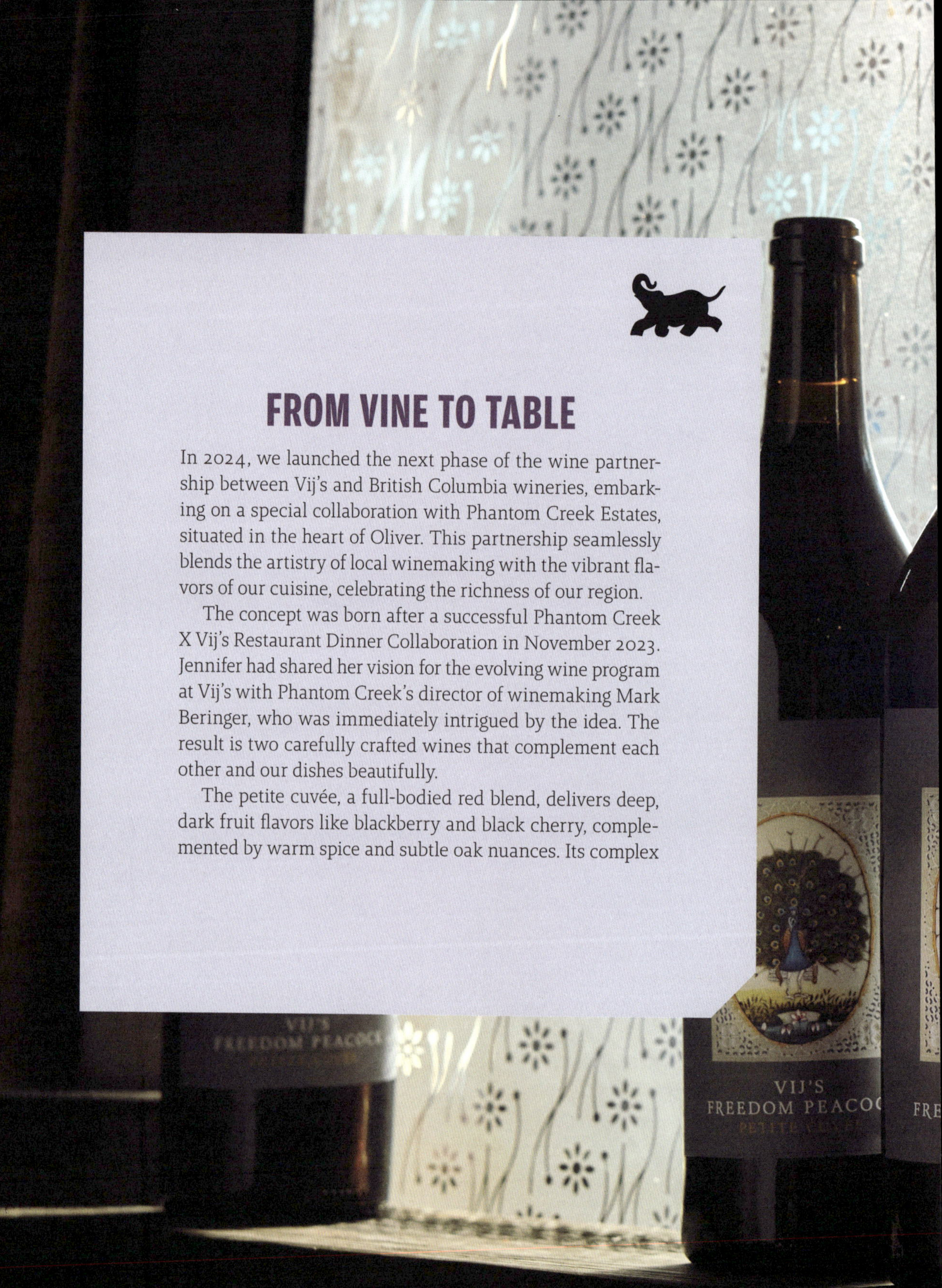

FROM VINE TO TABLE

In 2024, we launched the next phase of the wine partnership between Vij's and British Columbia wineries, embarking on a special collaboration with Phantom Creek Estates, situated in the heart of Oliver. This partnership seamlessly blends the artistry of local winemaking with the vibrant flavors of our cuisine, celebrating the richness of our region.

The concept was born after a successful Phantom Creek X Vij's Restaurant Dinner Collaboration in November 2023. Jennifer had shared her vision for the evolving wine program at Vij's with Phantom Creek's director of winemaking Mark Beringer, who was immediately intrigued by the idea. The result is two carefully crafted wines that complement each other and our dishes beautifully.

The petite cuvée, a full-bodied red blend, delivers deep, dark fruit flavors like blackberry and black cherry, complemented by warm spice and subtle oak nuances. Its complex

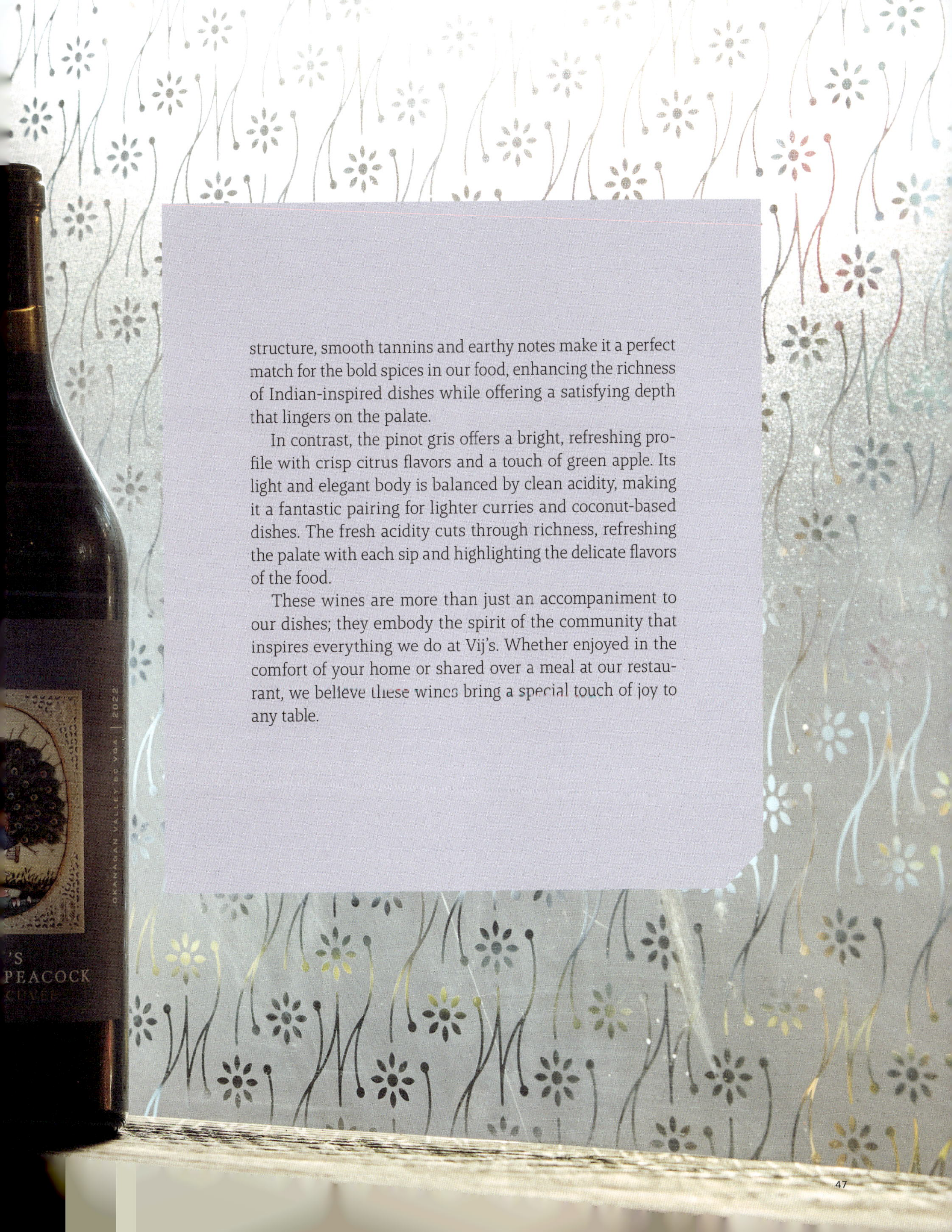

structure, smooth tannins and earthy notes make it a perfect match for the bold spices in our food, enhancing the richness of Indian-inspired dishes while offering a satisfying depth that lingers on the palate.

In contrast, the pinot gris offers a bright, refreshing profile with crisp citrus flavors and a touch of green apple. Its light and elegant body is balanced by clean acidity, making it a fantastic pairing for lighter curries and coconut-based dishes. The fresh acidity cuts through richness, refreshing the palate with each sip and highlighting the delicate flavors of the food.

These wines are more than just an accompaniment to our dishes; they embody the spirit of the community that inspires everything we do at Vij’s. Whether enjoyed in the comfort of your home or shared over a meal at our restaurant, we believe these wines bring a special touch of joy to any table.

<5 GF NF DF VEGAN

SERVES 1

This cocktail blends the smooth warmth of bourbon with the tropical sweetness of guava syrup and the bright zing of lemon juice. Topped with a float of fruity red wine, it offers a refreshing balance of bold, tangy and sweet notes. It's perfect for those who appreciate complex flavors and a touch of elegance in every sip.

Cambie Sour

- 1½ oz Buffalo Trace Bourbon
- 1 oz Giffard Guava Syrup or any tropical fruit syrup
- 1½ oz lemon juice
- 1½ oz fruity red wine (preferably Vij's Lantern Wine)

1. Add bourbon, syrup and lemon juice to a cocktail shaker.
2. Add ice to the shaker. Seal and shake vigorously for 20 seconds.
3. Strain into a rocks glass filled with ice.
4. Pour wine slowly over the back of a spoon into the glass so it floats on top.

SERVES 1

In July 2024, the Rolling Stones performed to a packed house at BC Place Stadium in Vancouver. People came from all over just to attend the show, making it an incredibly busy weekend at Vij's. That Saturday, Mick Jagger's assistant requested a table for six, along with a neighboring table for four security officers.

Accommodating them required a lot of juggling, and to make matters more challenging, I hadn't eaten anything all day, so my anxiety was through the roof. Thankfully, I learned they would be arriving late, which eased my mind, knowing the crowds would begin to thin out by then. Finally, at 9:45 pm, they arrived, and I was honored to serve them personally.

The energy in the restaurant and on the patio was electric as customers were thrilled to learn Mick Jagger was dining at Vij's. Mick was kind enough to take a picture with me and one of my team members, which made the moment even more special. After surviving the entire day on an empty stomach—just barely—I finally mustered enough energy to pour myself a large scotch, slump down on my couch and fall asleep. This cocktail was created in Mick Jagger's honor to commemorate his visit to Vij's.

You Can't Always Get What You Want

Honey syrup
2 Tbsp honey

Cocktail
2 oz scotch
1 oz Honey Syrup (see here)
1 oz lemon juice
Lemon twist, for garnish

Honey syrup

1. Combine honey and 1 tablespoon of water in a small bowl or glass and mix well.

Cocktail

2. Add scotch, syrup and lemon juice to a cocktail shaker.
3. Add ice to the shaker. Seal and shake vigorously for 5 seconds.
4. Strain into a chilled glass.
5. Garnish with the lemon twist.

VEGAN

SERVES 1

This cocktail is named after a beautiful Indian dancer as well as a famous Indian film. Served in a white bowl and topped with star anise, it's a fruity drink perfect for those who prefer something less alcohol-forward.

Anarkali

2 oz pineapple juice

1 oz anise-based liqueur, such as Pernod, Ricard Pastis or sambuca

1 oz lime juice

1 oz Giffard Passion Fruit Syrup, mango syrup or other fruit-forward syrup

1–2 oz club soda

1 star anise, for garnish

1. Add all ingredients, except for club soda and star anise, to a cocktail shaker.
2. Add ice to the shaker. Seal and shake vigorously for 5 seconds.
3. Strain into a broad glass or bowl.
4. Top with club soda. Garnish with star anise.

VEGAN

SERVES 1

I created this cocktail to honor the Indian soldiers who protect the country and its democracy. The drink blends the spicy aroma of garam masala, the invigorating mix of ginger and lemon, and the warmth of rum, which adds depth without overpowering the flavors. The dark rum specifically pays tribute to Old Monk, the popular Indian rum enjoyed by many of these soldiers.

This libation pairs beautifully with kebabs, grilled chicken and chutneys. Raise a glass to those who serve and protect.

Dark Army Cocktail

1½ oz Lemon Hart Rum
1 oz homemade or store-bought mango syrup, such as Giffard Mango Syrup
½ oz lemon juice
½ oz lime juice
1 tsp local bitters
4 oz ginger beer
Garam masala, for sprinkling

1. Fill a copper mug halfway with ice.
2. Add all liquid ingredients. Stir gently 3–4 times.
3. Sprinkle with garam masala.

BOUNTY OF THE EARTH

The Fraser Valley is truly a treasure, offering some of the freshest and most flavorful produce you'll find anywhere. With its fertile soil and sustainable farming practices, the region yields a remarkable variety of ingredients—from hearty root vegetables to fragrant herbs. What makes this bounty even more exceptional is the influence of the diverse immigrants who have settled here. Their cultural knowledge and passion for farming have enriched the land, enhancing its already abundant offerings.

SERVES 4

Many great Indian recipes are passed down through generations, and several of my favorites have been handed down to me. I've re-created them for this cookbook and truly hope I've done them justice.

This side dish, from Jennifer's grandmother, is simple to make and pairs wonderfully with Jennifer's Saltfish on page 109. Heirloom recipes are beautiful because they honor heritage, and this rice bake is a dish Jennifer fondly remembers from her childhood. It's also a great choice for young kids who aren't fans of too much spice.

Jennifer's Rice Bake

¼ cup (½ stick) + 2 Tbsp butter (divided)

½ onion, chopped (½ cup)

1 cup uncooked basmati rice

2 cups boiling chicken, beef or vegetable stock

1. Preheat oven to 350°F (180°C).
2. Heat ¼ cup of butter in a large frying pan over medium heat. Add onions and sauté for 3 minutes, until they are softened.
3. Add rice and stir to coat in butter. Pour in stock and stir well.
4. Transfer the mixture to a baking dish and cover. Bake for 20–25 minutes, until rice is tender and liquid is absorbed.
5. Gently mix in the remaining 2 tablespoons of butter. Serve immediately.

ALL SPICES MARKET
ALL
SPICES
MARKET
GINGER TEA
CARDAMOM TEA
MASALA TEA
Women Co-Oper
Society
SPICE TEA
KCF 2632

VEGAN

SERVES 4 (AS A SIDE DISH)

When I was once traveling in India, we had these delicious mustard potatoes with curry leaves. It's a simple yet flavorful side dish that works well with fish or meat.

Mustard Potatoes

- 4 Yukon Gold potatoes
- 2 Tbsp mustard oil
- 1 tsp mustard seeds
- 10–12 curry leaves
- 2 green bird's eye chilies, halved lengthwise
- 1 tsp ground turmeric
- Salt, to taste

LISTEN TO THE SOUNDS OF COOKING AND EATING

The sounds of food—whether it's the sizzling of ingredients in the pan or the satisfying crunch of fresh vegetables—can create an atmosphere that enhances the overall experience of eating.

1. Bring a saucepan of water to a boil. Add potatoes and boil for 15–20 minutes, until tender. Drain, then set aside to cool. When cool enough to handle, cut into 1½-inch cubes.
2. Heat oil in a frying pan over medium heat. Add mustard seeds and fry for 4 minutes, until they begin to sputter. Add curry leaves, chilies, turmeric and salt. Stir well.
3. Add potatoes and toss to coat. Cook for another 5–7 minutes, stirring occasionally.
4. Transfer to a serving plate and serve hot.

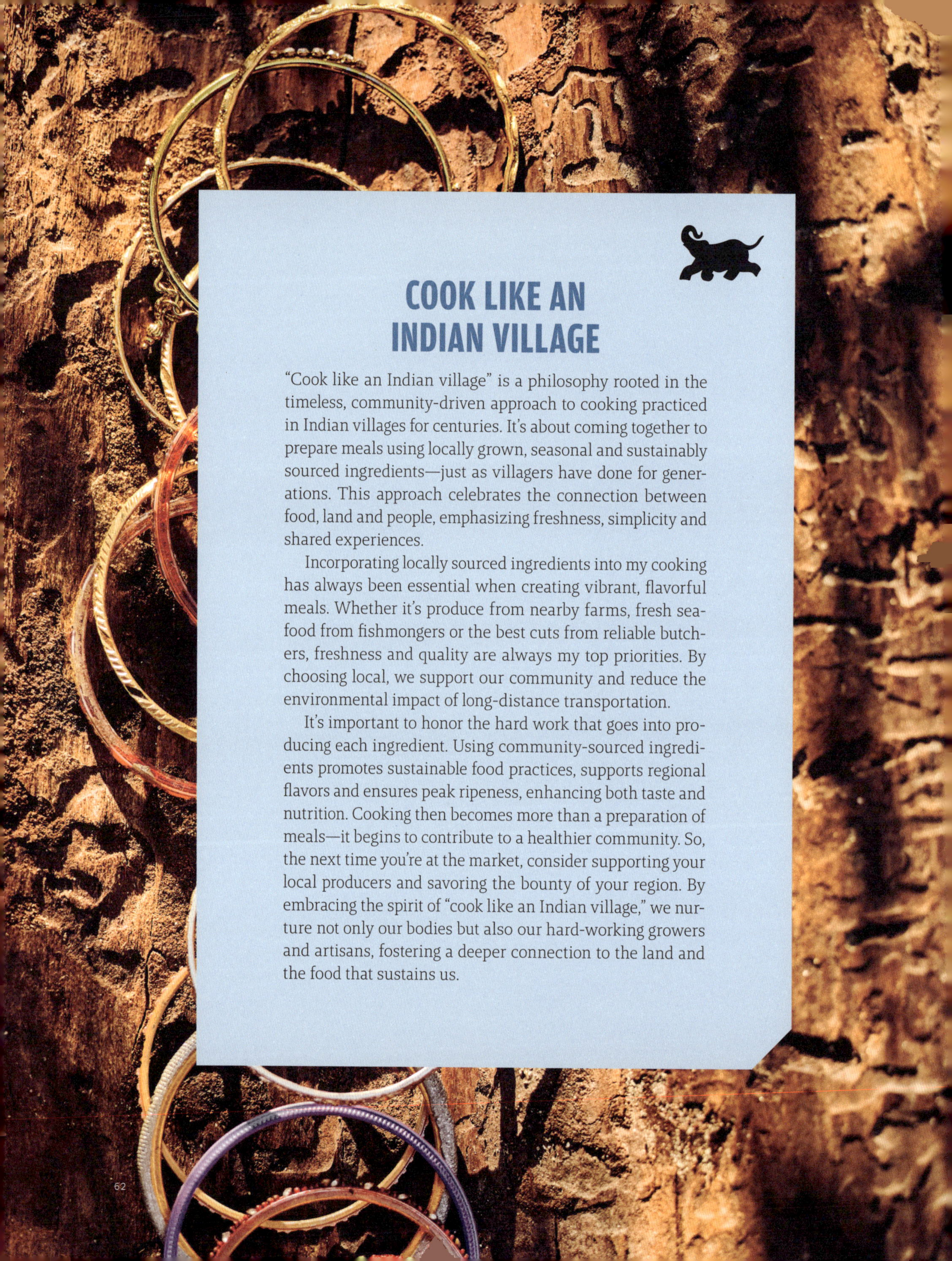

COOK LIKE AN INDIAN VILLAGE

"Cook like an Indian village" is a philosophy rooted in the timeless, community-driven approach to cooking practiced in Indian villages for centuries. It's about coming together to prepare meals using locally grown, seasonal and sustainably sourced ingredients—just as villagers have done for generations. This approach celebrates the connection between food, land and people, emphasizing freshness, simplicity and shared experiences.

Incorporating locally sourced ingredients into my cooking has always been essential when creating vibrant, flavorful meals. Whether it's produce from nearby farms, fresh seafood from fishmongers or the best cuts from reliable butchers, freshness and quality are always my top priorities. By choosing local, we support our community and reduce the environmental impact of long-distance transportation.

It's important to honor the hard work that goes into producing each ingredient. Using community-sourced ingredients promotes sustainable food practices, supports regional flavors and ensures peak ripeness, enhancing both taste and nutrition. Cooking then becomes more than a preparation of meals—it begins to contribute to a healthier community. So, the next time you're at the market, consider supporting your local producers and savoring the bounty of your region. By embracing the spirit of "cook like an Indian village," we nurture not only our bodies but also our hard-working growers and artisans, fostering a deeper connection to the land and the food that sustains us.

VEGETARIAN

SERVES 4

I love growing my own herbs in the summer. Each morning, I start with a cup of coffee, then talk to my plants and water them gently. Watching them thrive and follow their own paths reminds me that we should do the same—trust our hearts, dreams and passions. Only then can we truly find happiness and success.

Mint Chutney with Sour Cream

1 cup mint leaves
½ cup cilantro leaves
2 green chilies
1 clove garlic
1 tsp grated ginger
1 Tbsp lemon juice
Salt, to taste
½ cup sour cream
Parathas (page 84), to serve

1. Combine all ingredients, except sour cream, in a blender. Blend until smooth.
2. In a small bowl, mix the mint chutney with the sour cream. Refrigerate until chilled.
3. Serve as a dip with parathas.

VEGETARIAN

SERVES 4–6 (AS AN APPETIZER)

This refreshing and vibrant soup always impresses when served in a traditional Turkish bowl. My diners love the tableside presentation, which adds an element of mystery to the dish.

Chilled Pea Soup with Fried Mint

4 cups fresh or frozen peas
1 cup vegetable stock
1 cup heavy cream
Salt and pepper, to taste
1 Tbsp vegetable oil
Sprig of mint leaves

1. Bring a saucepan of water to a boil. Add peas and cook for 3–4 minutes. Drain, then plunge in ice water to cool. Drain again.
2. In a blender, combine peas, stock and cream and blend until smooth. Season with salt and pepper.
3. Chill soup in the fridge for at least 1 hour.
4. Heat oil in a small frying pan over medium heat. Add mint leaves and fry for 2 minutes, until crispy. Drain on a paper towel-lined plate.
5. Ladle the chilled soup into bowls. Garnish with the fried mint leaves.

SERVES 4

This twist on classic French onion soup is infused with Indian spices, giving it a unique flavor. Some people love it, while others are perplexed—but I don't mind challenging expectations with my cooking. For me, it's the freedom of personal expression that I cherish in the kitchen, turning my art into a plate of food.

Indian French Onion Soup

Croutons

4 cups cubed or sliced robust day-old bread, such as sourdough or baguette
6 Tbsp olive oil or melted butter
3 cloves garlic, finely chopped
1 tsp ground cumin
1 tsp garam masala
½ tsp salt
½ tsp pepper, or to taste

Soup

¼ cup (½ stick) butter
4 large onions, thinly sliced
2 cloves garlic, finely chopped
1 tsp ground cumin
1 tsp ground coriander
½ cup white wine
4 cups vegetable or chicken stock
Salt and pepper, to taste
1 cup grated Gruyère

Croutons

1. Preheat oven to 375°F (190°C).
2. In a large bowl, combine bread with oil (or melted butter) until evenly coated. Add garlic, cumin, garam masala, salt and pepper. Toss to coat.
3. Spread bread out in a single layer on a baking sheet. Bake for 10–15 minutes, stirring halfway through, until golden brown and crispy. Set aside to cool.

   Leftover croutons can be stored in an airtight container for up to a week.

Soup

4. Melt butter in a saucepan over medium heat. Add onions and garlic and sauté for 2 minutes, until translucent.
5. Add cumin and coriander and cook for another 3 minutes.
6. Pour in wine and simmer for 5–6 minutes, until reduced by half.
7. Add stock, then season with salt and pepper. Simmer, uncovered, for 20 minutes.
8. Top with grated Gruyère and croutons and serve hot.

VEGETARIAN

SERVES 4 (AS AN APPETIZER OR SIDE DISH)

Water buffalo milk cheese has a taste and texture very similar to feta. When combined with sweet tomatoes and herbaceous mint, it creates a deliciously vibrant salad that's both refreshing and satisfying, and the simple dressing of tangy lemon juice and olive oil brings everything together.

For an authentic touch, I like to serve this salad in a wooden bowl. Vancouver Island offers beautiful wooden bowls made from local arbutus trees—the wood's grain is simply gorgeous.

Paneer and Tomato Salad with Mint

1 small red onion, thinly sliced
2 cups sliced tomatoes
1 cup sliced water buffalo paneer
¼ cup mint leaves, chopped
2 Tbsp extra-virgin olive oil
1 Tbsp lemon juice
Salt and pepper, to taste

1. In a large bowl, combine onions, tomatoes, paneer and mint.
2. Drizzle with oil and lemon juice. Season with salt and pepper. Toss gently to combine and transfer to a wooden serving bowl.
3. Set aside for 30 minutes to intensify the flavor, then serve.

CHOOSE FRESH, LOCAL INGREDIENTS

Great cooking begins with fresh, high-quality ingredients. When you select the best local produce and meats, the natural flavors come through, making your dish shine with freshness and vibrancy.

VEGETARIAN

SERVES 4

This recipe calls for the freshest ingredients. While fresh paneer is essential, it's tedious to make and often difficult to find. Instead, I use burrata. It pairs beautifully with the delicious chutney made by cooking fresh mango in fragrant mustard oil along with salt, sugar and vinegar. I then add some fresh, ripe patio figs from the restaurant.

Burrata with Fig-Mango Chutney

7 oz (200 g) fresh soft paneer or burrata cheese
2 Tbsp mustard oil
1 ripe mango, chopped
2 Tbsp sugar
1 tsp salt
1 Tbsp white vinegar
4 ripe figs, chopped
Mint chutney, to serve (optional)

1. Place cheese in the center of a serving plate.
2. Heat oil in a frying pan over medium heat. Add mango, sugar, salt and vinegar and stir to mix. Sauté for 4–5 minutes, stirring occasionally, until it has a jam-like consistency.
3. Mix in figs and cook for 2 minutes, until softened.
4. Spoon the warm chutney over the cheese and serve immediately. If desired, pair with mint chutney.

   Leftover fig-mango chutney can be stored in an airtight container for up to 1 month in the fridge.

VEGETARIAN

SERVES 2–4

I love the combination of sweet watermelon and fried, spiced paneer with this spicy vinaigrette. The flavor and textural contrasts of this delightful dish make it a crowd-pleaser!

Watermelon and Paneer Masala with Spicy Vinaigrette

Fried paneer

1 Tbsp olive oil
1 cup cubed paneer
1 tsp garam masala
1 tsp red chili powder
1 tsp mango powder (*amchur*)

Spicy vinaigrette

¾ cup extra-virgin olive oil
¼ cup balsamic vinegar
1 tsp ground cumin
1 tsp ground coriander
1 tsp garam masala

Assembly

¼–½ watermelon, cut into 1-inch cubes (4 cups)
Cilantro leaves, for garnish
Naan bread or naan crisps, to serve (optional)

USE YOUR EYES TO APPRECIATE COLOR AND PRESENTATION

Before taking a bite, take time to appreciate the vibrant colors and thoughtful presentation of your food. The visual appeal of a dish can set the tone for the meal, enhancing the enjoyment from the very first glance.

Fried paneer

1. Heat oil in a frying pan over medium heat. Add paneer and fry for 2 minutes, until golden brown on all sides. Transfer paneer to a paper towel-lined plate to drain.
2. Sprinkle fried paneer with garam masala, chili powder and mango powder. Set aside.

Spicy vinaigrette

3. In a bowl, combine all ingredients and whisk until emulsified.

Assembly

4. On a long serving dish, alternate watermelon and paneer cubes like bricks.
5. Garnish with cilantro and drizzle vinaigrette on top. Serve immediately with fresh naan or naan crisps (if using)

VEGAN

SERVES 4

The first time I tasted this coconut-based chopped salad was in Kerala, South India. It brings back memories of my time at culinary school in Austria, where we often prepared delicious sauerkraut salads for the school kitchen. This salad makes a perfect vegetarian accompaniment to a meat or fish curry on hot summer nights.

Thoran Coleslaw (Not Your Regular Salad)

1 Tbsp vegetable oil
½ tsp mustard seeds
½ tsp cumin seeds
1 green bird's eye chili, finely chopped
¼ tsp ground turmeric
2 cups shredded cabbage
1 carrot, grated
½ cup freshly grated coconut
Salt, to taste
Juice of 1 lime
Chopped cilantro (optional)
Your favorite meat or fish curry, to serve (optional)

1. Heat oil in a frying pan over medium heat. Add mustard and cumin seeds and fry for 2 minutes, until they begin to sputter.
2. Stir in chili and turmeric. Add cabbage and carrot and sauté for 5–7 minutes, until slightly tender but still crisp.
3. Stir in coconut, season with salt and mix well. Remove from heat, then add lime juice.
4. Transfer to a serving plate, garnish with cilantro (if using) and serve alongside your favorite curry, if you like.

SERVES 4–6

This stand-out vegetarian salad is a flavorful fusion of fresh vegetables, tangy feta cheese and aromatic Indian spices, and is a refreshing and versatile side suited to accompanying a light main course. Feel free to adjust the heat to suit your personal preference by reducing or increasing the amount of chili powder—you want to create a balanced flavor of sweetness, creaminess and spice.

Spiced Feta and Corn Salad

Salad

2 cups fresh or frozen corn kernels
1 cup cherry tomatoes, halved
1 cucumber, diced
1 red bell pepper, seeded, deveined and diced
½ red onion, finely chopped
½ cup crumbled feta cheese
¼ cup chopped cilantro
¼ cup chopped mint

Dressing

3 Tbsp olive oil
2 Tbsp lime juice
1 Tbsp honey
1 tsp ground cumin
½ tsp ground coriander
½ tsp garam masala
¼–½ tsp red chili powder, to taste
¼ tsp ground turmeric
Salt and pepper, to taste

MAKE RECIPES YOUR OWN

Feel free to personalize your dishes. Add your twist to a family classic or create something entirely new. Bringing your own story or memories into the recipe adds depth and meaning to every bite.

Salad

1. Bring a saucepan of water to a boil. Add corn and cook for 2–3 minutes, until tender. Drain, then let cool. (If using frozen corn, thaw and drain well.)
2. Combine all salad ingredients in a large bowl and mix well.

Dressing

3. Whisk all ingredients in a bowl until well combined.

Assembly

4. Pour dressing over salad and gently toss to coat.
5. Set aside for 10 minutes to allow flavors to meld. Serve chilled or at room temperature.

SERVES 4

This vibrant beetroot salad blends the natural sweetness of beets with a tangy and spiced yogurt dressing. Enhanced with toasted cumin seeds, fresh mint and tart pomegranate seeds, it's a medley of colors, flavors and textures that can be served as a refreshing side dish or a light main course.

Beetroot Salad with Spiced Yogurt Dressing

- 3 beets
- 1 cup plain yogurt
- 1 Tbsp lemon juice
- 1 tsp ground cumin
- 1 tsp chaat masala
- Salt, to taste
- 1 green bird's eye chili, finely chopped (optional)
- 1 Tbsp chopped mint leaves, plus extra for garnish
- 1 Tbsp chopped cilantro leaves, plus extra for garnish
- 2 small shallots, thinly sliced
- 2 Tbsp pomegranate seeds
- 2 Tbsp crushed toasted peanuts (optional)
- 1 tsp cumin seeds, toasted

1. Bring a saucepan of water to a boil. Add beets and boil for 15 minutes, until tender. Drain, then set aside to cool. When cool enough to handle, cut into 1-inch square slices.
2. Whisk yogurt in a bowl until smooth. Add lemon juice, ground cumin, chaat masala and salt. Mix well.
3. Add beets to the yogurt dressing and toss to evenly coat. Stir in chilies (if using), mint and cilantro.
4. Transfer salad to a serving dish. Garnish with shallots, pomegranate seeds and peanuts (if using). Refrigerate until chilled.
5. Garnish with more mint and cilantro, sprinkle with toasted cumin seeds and serve.

VEGETARIAN

SERVES 4

This fantastic salad is a feast for the senses, combining juicy tomatoes, sweet cherries, and fragrant basil with creamy burrata and crispy shards of burnt brown sugar. It shines in the summer when seasonal ingredients are at their peak, delivering the freshest and most vibrant flavors. Best of all, and despite its complex taste, it is quick to prepare and effortlessly impressive—it is the perfect dish for entertaining guests.

Cherry, Burrata and Tomato Salad with Burnt Brown Sugar

Burnt brown sugar

¼ cup brown sugar

Salad

1 pint cherry tomatoes, halved

1 cup cherries, pitted and halved

8 oz room-temperature burrata cheese, drained

2 Tbsp extra-virgin olive oil

1 Tbsp balsamic glaze

Salt and pepper, to taste

¼ cup basil leaves, torn

Handful of arugula or baby spinach, for garnish (optional)

Burnt brown sugar

1. In a small saucepan, combine brown sugar and 1 teaspoon of water. Stir over medium heat until sugar has dissolved. Leave untouched and cook for another 2 minutes, until caramelized and deep amber in color. Do not let it burn. (Remove pan from heat, if necessary.)
2. Pour onto a baking sheet lined with parchment paper and set aside to cool completely and harden. Break into small shards.

Salad

3. On a large serving plate or in a salad bowl, arrange tomatoes and cherries. Tear burrata into pieces and place them randomly around the tomatoes and cherries.
4. Drizzle oil and balsamic glaze over salad. Season to taste with salt and pepper.
5. Top with shards of burnt brown sugar and torn basil leaves. Garnish with arugula or baby spinach (if using) at the edges.
6. Serve immediately.

VEGETARIAN

SERVES 4

The Persian poet Amir Khusrau once said, "If there is paradise, it is right here, in the valley of Kashmir." With its stunning mountains and lakes and a cuisine influenced by the bordering countries of Pakistan and Afghanistan, Kashmir is an incredible (and scenic) food destination.

Inspired by this beautiful northern Indian state, these delicious parathas are uniquely flavored with dates and raisins. And when I crave something more savory, I enjoy the parathas alongside a condiment made with yogurt, onions, cilantro and cumin seeds.

Kashmiri Fruit Parathas

Parathas

2 cups whole-wheat flour

½ tsp salt

½ cup warm milk

Filling

½ cup chopped dates

½ cup raisins

¼ cup chopped almonds and/or cashews

½ tsp ground cinnamon

¼ tsp ground cardamom

1 Tbsp ghee

Parathas

1 In a mixing bowl, combine flour and salt.

2 Gradually add milk and knead mixture into a soft dough. Cover, then set aside for 30 minutes.

Filling

3 Combine all ingredients, except ghee, in a bowl.

Assembly

4 Divide the paratha dough into 4 small balls. Flatten each ball, to about ½ inch thick, and divide the filling between the centers.

5 Fold dough over filling and roll it out gently, until about ½ inch thick.

6 Heat ghee in a frying pan over medium heat. Add parathas one at a time and fry for 3 minutes on each side, until golden brown.

7 Serve warm.

VEGETARIAN

SERVES 4

Soft, warm naan provides the perfect vehicle for a creative mix of toppings, transforming the flatbread into a flavorful and customizable dish. Sometimes, when I make fresh naan, I use the leftovers to create naan pizza topped with mushrooms, bell peppers, korma sauce, paneer and cilantro. It's now a popular top seller and family-favorite dish at the restaurant.

Naan Pizza

¼ cup Korma Sauce (page 135)
1 naan bread
½ cup sliced mushrooms
½ cup sliced bell peppers
½ cup grated paneer
Cilantro, for garnish

1. Preheat oven to 375°F (190°C).
2. Spread korma sauce over naan. Top with mushrooms, bell peppers and paneer.
3. Bake for 10–12 minutes, until the naan is crispy and the paneer is soft.
4. Garnish with cilantro and serve.

FEEL THE TEXTURES

Experience the texture of your food, whether it's the crunch of a perfectly fried crust or the smoothness of a rich sauce. These tactile sensations add another layer of pleasure to the meal.

SERVES 4

Aloo gobi is a classic Indian dish made with tender potatoes (*aloo*) and cauliflower (*gobi*) cooked in a fragrant blend of spices. Here, I've used the savory spiced vegetables in parathas to create a satisfying dish that would be perfect paired with a homemade mango or berry lassi (pages 33 and 30, respectively). It also makes a great addition to a brunch with family and friends.

Aloo Gobi Parathas

2 cups whole-wheat flour, plus extra for dusting
½ tsp salt, plus extra to taste
½ cup milk
½ cup mashed potatoes
½ cup grated cauliflower
1 tsp cumin seeds
1 tsp ground turmeric
Vegetable oil or ghee, for frying

1. Combine flour and salt in a bowl. Gradually add milk to form a sticky dough and knead until soft. Transfer dough to a clean work surface lightly dusted with flour. Knead for 5 minutes, until soft.
2. In a separate bowl, combine mashed potatoes, cauliflower, cumin seeds and turmeric. Season with salt.
3. Divide dough into 4 balls and stuff each ball with 1 tablespoon of the potato-cauliflower mixture. Leftover filling can be stored in an airtight container for up to a week in the fridge.
4. Using a rolling pin, roll out each ball into a flat disk, about ½ inch thick.
5. Heat oil (or ghee) on a hot griddle over medium heat. Add parathas one at a time and fry for 3–4 minutes on each side, until golden brown.

 VEGETARIAN

SERVES 2

In 1994, I opened my first restaurant in a space that had previously housed a Lebanese restaurant. While I revamped the restaurant to serve Indian food, I wanted to preserve the location's heritage in some way. (Many people in the Indian community were surprised by this decision, as it is customary to take over a kitchen of the same cuisine.)

The result was this fusion dish, blending Lebanese and Indian elements: a pan-fried pita stuffed with a flavorful potato filling, served with a sour cream–fenugreek dipping sauce. It represents the freedom and creativity I cherish in both my cooking and personal journey, where I can break free from convention and experiment with new ingredients to experience all the flavors the world has to offer.

Spiced Potato in Pita Bread with Sour Cream–Fenugreek Dip

2 large potatoes, peeled and halved
2 Tbsp vegetable oil (divided)
1 tsp cumin seeds
1 tsp ground turmeric
1 tsp garam masala
Salt, to taste
2 pita pockets, halved
½ cup sour cream
1 Tbsp dried fenugreek leaves

1. Bring a saucepan of water to a boil. Add potatoes and boil for 10–15 minutes, until tender. Drain, then set aside to cool. When cool enough to handle, cut into ½-inch cubes.
2. Heat 1 tablespoon of oil in a frying pan. Add cumin seeds and fry for 3 minutes, until they begin to sputter. Add turmeric, garam masala and potatoes. Stir well, then fry for 5 minutes. Season to taste with salt.
3. Open the pita pockets. Stuff them with the spiced potatoes.
4. Heat the remaining tablespoon of oil in a frying pan over medium heat. Pan-fry the stuffed pita pockets for 2 minutes, until golden brown and crispy.
5. In a small bowl, combine sour cream and fenugreek leaves and mix well.
6. To serve, transfer the stuffed pita pockets to a serving plate. Serve with the sour cream–fenugreek dip.

SERVES 2

I perfected my rösti-making skills while studying in Austria, and I love incorporating the dish into my cooking. Serving it in the pan not only gives the rösti an authentic look but also enhances its incredible flavor.

Rösti with Portobello Mushrooms

- 4 russet potatoes, peeled and grated
- 2 Tbsp olive oil (divided)
- 2 large portobello mushrooms, sliced
- 1 tsp garam masala
- Salt and pepper, to taste
- ½ cup vegetable stock
- ¼ cup heavy cream

1. Drain water out of grated potatoes by pressing them with a paper towel.
2. Heat 1 tablespoon of oil in a cast-iron frying pan over medium heat. Add grated potatoes, spreading them out and flattening them with a spatula to form an even layer. Cook for 3–4 minutes on one side, until golden brown. Carefully flip and fry for another 3 minutes, until crispy and cooked through. Set pan with rösti aside.
3. Heat the remaining tablespoon of oil in a frying pan over medium heat. Add mushrooms and sauté for 3 minutes, until they start to soften. Add garam masala, season with salt and pepper, and cook for 2 minutes, until mushrooms are tender.
4. Scatter mushrooms over the rösti, like a pizza topping.
5. Pour stock into the same pan used to cook the mushrooms and deglaze over medium heat, scraping up any browned bits. Pour in cream and simmer for 4 minutes, until sauce is thickened and reduced.
6. Pour the sauce over the mushrooms and rösti. Serve hot in the pan.

VEGAN

SERVES 4

British Columbia is home to some of the best mushroom farms, offering a wide variety of fresh mushrooms, and this earthy dish wonderfully bridges French and Indian culinary traditions. Robust portobellos are the perfect choice for this green coconut curry, staying firm while soaking up all the rich, aromatic flavors. Whether enjoyed as a warming soup or a hearty vegetarian meal, it's best served with naan to soak up every last bit of that flavorful sauce.

Mushroom Curry

- Vegetable oil, for frying
- 1 onion, finely chopped
- 2 green bird's eye chilies, chopped
- 2 cloves garlic, finely chopped
- ½ Tbsp grated ginger
- 2 Tbsp green curry paste
- 1 lb portobello mushrooms, sliced
- 1 bell pepper, seeded, deveined and sliced
- 1 zucchini, sliced
- 1 (14-oz/400-mL) can coconut milk
- 1 Tbsp soy sauce
- 1 Tbsp lime juice
- Salt, to taste
- Cilantro, for garnish
- Naan or rice, to serve

1. Heat oil in a large saucepan over medium heat. Add onions and sauté for 2 minutes, until softened and translucent. Add chilies, garlic and ginger. Sauté for another 2–3 minutes.
2. Stir in curry paste and cook for another minute.
3. Add mushrooms, bell peppers and zucchini and sauté for 2 minutes, until the vegetables are softened.
4. Pour in coconut milk and soy sauce. Simmer for 10–15 minutes, until flavors meld.
5. Stir in lime juice. Season to taste with salt.
6. Garnish with cilantro, then serve hot with naan or rice.

VEGAN

SERVES 4

Jennifer and I had this dish at a restaurant in Jaipur and we loved the idea of this quick and simple side. Baby eggplants are pan-fried with aromatic spices, but you can easily substitute them with brussels sprouts or regular eggplants, though they will need a longer cooking time.

Spiced Baby Eggplant

2 Tbsp vegetable oil
1 tsp cumin seeds
1 tsp mustard seeds
1 lb baby eggplants, halved lengthwise
1 tsp ground turmeric
1 tsp ground coriander
1 tsp garam masala
Salt, to taste
Cilantro, for garnish

1. Heat oil in a frying pan over medium heat. Add cumin and mustard seeds and fry for 2 minutes, until they begin to sputter.
2. Add baby eggplants and sauté for 5 minutes. Add turmeric, coriander, garam masala and salt. Sauté for another 2–3 minutes, until eggplants are tender and coated in the spices.
3. Garnish with cilantro and serve hot.

VEGAN

SERVES 4 (AS A SNACK OR APPETIZER)

Infused with bold Indian spices like cumin, turmeric, coriander and chili powder, these crispy cauliflower fritters are a perfect balance of crunchy exterior and tender cauliflower inside. Plus, they are easy to prepare with simple ingredients—super accessible to any cook. A versatile vegetarian option, they make a fantastic snack or impressive appetizer for gatherings.

Spiced Cauliflower Fritters

1 cauliflower, cut into bite-sized florets

1 cup chickpea flour (*besan*)

½ cup rice flour or all-purpose flour

1 tsp cumin seeds

1 tsp ground cumin

1 tsp ground coriander

1 tsp ground turmeric

¼–½ tsp red chili powder, to taste

Salt, to taste

Vegetable oil, for deep-frying

Cilantro leaves, for garnish

Favorite dipping sauce or chutney, to serve

1. Rinse cauliflower florets under cold water and pat dry with a paper towel.
2. In a large bowl, combine both flours and all the spices. Gradually pour in ½ cup of water, stirring continuously until batter is thick and smooth. If it's too thick, add up to another ¼ cup of water.
3. Pour oil into a deep fryer or deep saucepan and heat to a temperature of 350°F–375°F (177°C–190°C). Dip cauliflower florets into the batter, ensuring they're well coated. Working in batches to avoid overcrowding, carefully lower cauliflower into pan, taking care not to splash hot oil. Deep-fry for 4–5 minutes, turning occasionally, until golden brown and crispy.
4. Using a slotted spoon, transfer the fritters to a paper towel-lined plate to drain. Repeat with the remaining batches.
5. Garnish with cilantro and serve hot with your favorite dipping sauce or chutney.

VEGETARIAN

SERVES 4–6

Gnocchi's soft, pillowy texture makes it a perfect base for absorbing bold, aromatic Indian spices, allowing their flavors to truly shine and creating a satisfying contrast. You can find quality pre-made gnocchi at specialty stores or you can make it yourself (though it takes more time). The key is to prepare the masala from scratch and serve while the paneer is hot and crispy.

Gnocchi with Garam Masala Tomato Sauce and Paneer

Tomato sauce

Olive oil, for frying
1 large onion, finely chopped
3 cloves garlic, finely chopped
1 Tbsp grated ginger
4 ripe tomatoes, chopped
2 tsp garam masala
1 tsp ground turmeric
Salt and pepper, to taste

Gnocchi

1 (1-lb) package store-bought or homemade gnocchi

Assembly

Olive oil, for greasing
1 cup grated paneer
Chopped basil, for garnish

Tomato sauce

1. Heat oil in a saucepan over medium heat. Add onions, garlic and ginger and sauté for 3 minutes, until onions are golden brown.
2. Add tomatoes and cook for another 15 minutes, stirring occasionally, until tomatoes break down and form a thick sauce. Add garam masala and turmeric. Season with salt and pepper. Stir, then cook for another 5–7 minutes, until flavors meld together.

Gnocchi

3. Bring a large saucepan of salted water to a boil. Add gnocchi and cook according to package instructions. (They will float to the surface once cooked.) Drain, then set aside.

Assembly

4. Preheat oven to 300°F (150°C). Grease a baking dish with oil.
5. Add the cooked gnocchi and toss gently to coat them in the oil. Pour in the sauce, ensuring gnocchi are evenly covered.
6. Sprinkle paneer on top, then bake for 20 minutes.
7. Increase heat to the broil setting and broil for 3 minutes, until paneer is golden brown and crispy.
8. Garnish with basil and serve hot.

VEGETARIAN

SERVES 6

Dhaal is a highly nutritious and satisfying staple in every household, cherished by all—from young to old, everyone enjoys a warm bowl of dhaal. In India, the types of dhaals are as diverse as the spices that flavor them, each one unique and full of character.

This version, perfected by Jennifer's grandmother, is versatile with universal appeal. If I could make a request for my final meal, it would be this dish, accompanied with a nice bottle of sauvignon blanc or pinot noir—just because we love those two grape varietals so much.

A Mother's Dhaal

- 1 cup yellow pigeon peas (*toor dhaal*)
- 1 tsp ground turmeric
- Pinch of salt
- 1 Tbsp vegetable oil or ghee
- 1 tsp cumin seeds
- 1 tsp mustard seeds
- ½–1 tsp red chili powder, to taste
- 1 tsp garam masala
- 1 onion, finely chopped
- 1 tomato, chopped
- 2–3 cloves garlic, finely chopped
- ½ Tbsp grated ginger
- 1–2 green chilies, chopped
- Cilantro leaves, chopped, for garnish

1. Rinse pigeon peas (dhaal) thoroughly under cold running water. Combine dhaal and 3 cups of water in a pressure cooker. Add turmeric and salt. Cook at medium heat for 3–4 whistles, until dhaal is soft and fully cooked. Using the back of a spoon or a masher, mash dhaal slightly. Set aside.
2. Heat oil (or ghee) in a frying pan over medium heat. Add the remaining spices and cook for 1–2 minutes. (This is known as *tadka*.) Add onions, tomatoes, garlic, ginger and chilies and fry for 3–4 minutes, until the vegetables soften. Pour this mixture over the dhaal. Garnish with cilantro, then serve.

REINVENT COMFORT FOOD

Sometimes cooking from the heart means preparing comforting, nostalgic meals that warm the soul. It's about the emotional connection food creates, reminding us of home, family and happiness.

 VEGETARIAN

SERVES 4–6

Dhaal makhaani, meaning "creamy and soft-as-butter dhaal," is a popular lentil dish from North India. This is my indulgent take on the traditional recipe. With its rich, creamy texture and robust flavors, it makes for a hearty and comforting meal that pairs nicely with a refreshing lassi, such as the Mango Lassi on page 33.

Northern-Style Dhaal Makhaani

1 cup black gram (*urad dhaal*)
¼ cup red kidney beans (*rajma*)
Pinch of salt, plus extra to taste
2 Tbsp ghee or butter
1 tsp cumin seeds
1 large onion, finely chopped
1 Tbsp ginger-garlic paste
1 green bird's eye chili, finely chopped (optional)
2 tomatoes, finely chopped
1 tsp red chili powder
1 tsp ground coriander
1 tsp garam masala
½ tsp ground turmeric
½ cup whipping cream
Cilantro leaves, for garnish
Rice or naan, to serve

1. Combine black gram and kidney beans in a colander and thoroughly rinse under cold running water. Place them in a bowl with 4 cups of water. Set aside to soak for at least 6 hours, or overnight.
2. Drain, then transfer to a pressure cooker or a large saucepan. Add 4 cups of fresh water and a pinch of salt. If using a pressure cooker, cook for 4–5 whistles, until pulses are soft and fully cooked. (Alternatively, if cooking them in a saucepan on the stovetop, cover and simmer for 1 hour.) Using the back of a spoon or a masher, mash the gram and beans slightly. Set aside.
3. Heat ghee (or butter) in a frying pan over medium heat. Add cumin seeds and fry for 2 minutes, until they begin to sputter. Add onions and sauté for 3–4 minutes, until golden.
4. Add ginger-garlic paste and chilies (if using) and sauté for 1 minute, until fragrant. Add tomatoes and cook for 4 minutes, until tomatoes are softened and the oil separates from the masala.
5. Stir in chili powder, coriander, garam masala and turmeric.
6. Add the cooked gram and beans and stir well to combine. Stir in cream. If necessary, thin out the dhaal with water.
7. Simmer for 10–15 minutes over low heat, stirring occasionally, to allow the flavors to meld together. Season to taste with salt and spices.
8. Garnish with cilantro and serve hot with rice or naan.

COASTAL FLAVORS

Vancouver and its surrounding waters boast one of the most vibrant and sustainable fishing communities, offering everything from spotted prawns and halibut to crab, salmon, mussels and oysters. I've always believed in respecting the ocean, which is why local seafood has a special place on my menu. I love pairing these fresh ingredients with the coastal curries of India, especially with coconut milk for its unique texture. Adding a touch of Indian spices makes each dish truly my own—distinct, flavorful and unmistakably Vij's.

SERVES 4 (AS AN APPETIZER)

The first time I tasted a truly great ceviche was in Mexico City, where I was invited by the Canadian government to explore the connections between Indian and Mexican cuisine. (For example, tomatoes and cilantro, now staples in Indian cooking, were introduced through trade.)

One day, while nursing a serious tequila hangover, I wandered into a local market and tried homemade shrimp ceviche with taco chips. The fresh, vibrant flavors and tangy acidity were incredibly refreshing. I later adapted the dish using albacore tuna, though any white fish will soak up the bright flavors of lime, cilantro and tomatoes beautifully.

Tuna Ceviche

- 1 lb fresh quality tuna, cut into ½-inch cubes
- 1 cup lime juice
- 1 tomato, chopped
- 1 small red onion, finely chopped
- 1 jalapeño, seeded, deveined and finely chopped
- ½ cup chopped cilantro, plus extra for garnish
- Salt and pepper, to taste
- Tortilla chips, to serve

1. In a large bowl, combine tuna and lime juice. Cover and refrigerate for 1 hour.
2. Drain tuna, then mix it with tomatoes, red onions, jalapeño and cilantro. Season with salt and pepper. Refrigerate until chilled.
3. Garnish with a small cilantro sprig. Serve with tortilla chips.

SERVES 4

Chefs often say that salmon should be prepared delicately to highlight its unique flavor, and while I agree with that, I also like to challenge it. Garam masala works wonders, and many people love the combination of flavors in this dish. It's a beautiful fusion of BC's rich seafood bounty and my Indian heritage.

The First Nations people were the original salmon harvesters, and thanks to them, we continue to enjoy this incredible fish. Ha7lh n skwálwen kwis tl'iknumut (Glad you could be here, in the Sḵwx̱wú7mesh language) and namaste—I honor you and the energy within you, in Hindi.

Spiced Pan-Seared Salmon with Herbs

2 (6-oz) skin-on salmon fillets
Salt and pepper, to taste
1 Tbsp garam masala
½ tsp cumin seeds, crushed
¼ tsp ground turmeric
1 Tbsp vegetable oil
1 Tbsp butter
1 lemon, cut into wedges
¼ cup chopped cilantro, for garnish
¼ cup chopped dill, for garnish

1. Pat salmon fillets dry with a paper towel. Season both sides with salt and pepper.
2. In a small bowl, combine garam masala, cumin and turmeric. Sprinkle this spice blend over the flesh side of the salmon, pressing gently to help it adhere.
3. Heat oil in a large skillet over medium-high heat. Add salmon fillets, skin side down, then add butter to the pan and baste the salmon with it right away. Cook for 4–5 minutes, basting occasionally, until skin is crispy and the fillets are 70% cooked through. (Just make sure the spices remain on the top.)
4. Transfer fillets to a serving plate, skin side down, and set aside to rest for 1 minute. Squeeze fresh lemon juice overtop and garnish with cilantro and dill. Serve with the remaining lemon wedges.

SERVES 4

When I was growing up in Amritsar, I remember going with my aunt to a small local spot famous for its fried fish. It was a hot evening, and with a few roadside stands around, we grabbed our fish wrapped in newspaper and sat on the bonnet of the car to enjoy it—something locals, me included, often did. This dish holds a special place in my heart and is a fond memory of my childhood. I hope you enjoy it as much as I do.

Ling Cod in Coconut Curry

1 lb ling cod fillets
1 tsp salt
1 tsp ground turmeric
1 cup rice flour
2 Tbsp vegetable oil (divided)
10–12 curry leaves
1 tsp mustard seeds
2 green bird's eye chilies, halved lengthwise
1 onion, finely chopped
2 tomatoes, puréed
1 tsp ground coriander
1 tsp ground cumin
1 cup coconut milk
Rice, to serve

1. Season ling cod with salt and turmeric. Dredge fillets in rice flour.
2. Heat 1 tablespoon of oil in a large frying pan over medium heat. Add fillets and fry for 2 minutes on each side, until golden and crisp. Set aside.
3. Heat another tablespoon of oil in a separate frying pan. Add curry leaves and mustard seeds and fry for 2 minutes, until the mustard seeds sputter. Add chilies and onions and sauté for 3 minutes, until onions are golden brown.
4. Add tomato purée, coriander and cumin and cook for another 5–7 minutes. Pour in coconut milk and simmer for another 5 minutes.
5. Add the fried fillets and simmer for 2–3 minutes, to heat through.
6. Serve hot with rice.

SERVES 4

I use cod trimmings and smaller pieces from my main dishes to make these popular pakoras at my restaurant. Paired with pickled onions, green chutney and a sprinkle of homemade chaat masala, they're always a hit—it's nearly impossible to stop at just one!

Spicy Cod Pakoras

- Vegetable oil, for deep frying
- 1 cup chickpea flour (*besan*)
- 1 tsp ground cumin
- 1 tsp ground coriander
- ½ tsp ground turmeric
- ½ tsp red chili powder
- ½ tsp garam masala
- ½ tsp salt
- ¼ tsp baking soda
- 1 lb cod or any firm white fish, cut into bite-sized pieces
- Chaat masala, for sprinkling
- Pickled onions and green chutney, to serve

1. Pour oil into a deep fryer or deep saucepan and heat to a temperature of 350°F (177°C).
2. In a large bowl, combine chickpea flour, cumin, coriander, turmeric, chili powder, garam masala, salt and baking soda.
3. Gradually add enough water to make a thick and smooth batter. Dip the pieces of cod into the batter, coating them well.
4. Working in batches to avoid overcrowding, carefully lower battered cod into the hot oil, taking care not to splash it. Deep-fry for 4–5 minutes, until golden brown and crispy. Drain on a paper towel–lined plate.
5. Sprinkle with chaat masala and serve hot with pickled onions and green chutney.

SERVES 4

BC halibut farming is something we're truly proud of—it's not only sustainable and highly regulated, but it's also a favorite of chefs around the world. This firm, versatile white fish shines in so many dishes, whether it's served in a fresh ceviche, a hearty bouillabaisse or tucked into flavorful Mexican tacos.

Take this Pistachio-Crusted Halibut, for instance—its blend of Indian spices and French-style presentation highlights just how adaptable and delicious BC halibut can be.

Pistachio-Crusted Halibut

½ cup shelled pistachios, chopped
1 tsp garam masala
½ tsp ground coriander
¼ tsp ground turmeric
¼ tsp ground cumin
Salt and pepper, to taste
4 (6-oz) halibut fillets
1 Tbsp olive oil, plus extra for brushing
¼ cup chopped cilantro, for garnish
4 lemon wedges, to serve

1. In a small bowl, combine pistachios, garam masala, coriander, turmeric, cumin, salt and pepper. Mix well.
2. Pat halibut fillets dry with a paper towel. Lightly brush both sides of each fillet with oil. Press the pistachio mixture onto the top side of each fillet to form a crust.
3. Heat 1 tablespoon of oil in a nonstick frying pan over medium heat. Add fillets, crust side down, and cook for 3–4 minutes, until the crust is golden and slightly crisp. Carefully flip fillets and cook for another 2–3 minutes, until fish is cooked through and flakes easily with a fork. Set aside to rest for 2 minutes.
4. Garnish with cilantro and serve with lemon wedges on the side.

THE DOOR THAT HOLDS A THOUSAND STORIES

The hand-carved door at Vij's is seven hundred years old, made of Himalayan teak, and weighs a thousand pounds. It's a stunning focal point of the restaurant and exudes a natural, positive energy.

I acquired this remarkable work of art from a couple who were regulars at the restaurant. The door cost US$10,000, so I negotiated to pay $100 a month, which was all I could afford at the time. Over the years, I've written many cheques to pay it off, but it's been worth every penny.

The door is now a beloved feature of the restaurant, and I truly believe it brings positive energy to everyone who touches it. It is proudly displayed at my new location on Cambie Street, where it continues to radiate a subtle yet powerful vibe.

SERVES 4

Saltfish is fish—typically cod—that has been dried and salted, giving it a firm texture and a bold, distinctive flavor. It is a staple ingredient in Caribbean, African and South Asian cuisines and is widely available at specialty grocery stores and international markets.

Jennifer's grandmother prepares a simple yet deeply flavorful saltfish dish, and I'm honored to share her cherished family recipe in this cookbook. For a perfect pairing, try it with Jennifer's Rice Bake (page 58).

Jennifer's Saltfish

1 lb saltfish, skin on and bone in
2 tsp vegetable oil
1 onion, chopped coarsely
2 tomatoes, sliced
Lemon juice or hot sauce, to taste

1. Rinse saltfish under cold running water.
2. Bring a saucepan of water to a boil. Add fish, reduce heat to low and simmer for 10 minutes, until the skin begins to separate.
3. Drain fish, then rinse under cold running water. Remove skin, then rinse again. Set aside in a bowl.
4. Heat oil in a frying pan over medium heat. Add onions and sauté for 3 minutes, until softened. Add tomatoes and cook for another 3 minutes, until they begin to soften. Add saltfish and fry until warmed through. The saltfish will break apart in the pan and combine well with the onions and tomatoes.
5. Season to taste with lemon juice or hot sauce. Serve warm.

SERVES 4

BC is renowned for its large spot prawns, available from mid-May to July. The Spot Prawn Festival, run by the Chef's Table Society of BC, has been a popular event since my time as president. I once prepared this dish for thousands at an event supporting sustainable seafood. Boats would dock to sell us their fresh catch, reminding me of the importance of championing our oceans, our fisheries and the communities that provide us with such high-quality products.

Spot Prawns with Garlic, Ginger and Cumin

- 2 Tbsp olive oil
- 1 tsp cumin seeds
- 4 cloves garlic, finely chopped
- 1 Tbsp grated ginger
- 1 lb spot prawns, peeled and deveined
- Salt, to taste
- Cilantro, for garnish
- Lemon wedges, to serve

1. Heat oil in a frying pan over medium heat. Add cumin seeds and fry for 2 minutes, until they begin to sputter. Add garlic and ginger and sauté for 2–3 minutes until fragrant.
2. Add spot prawns and sauté for 5 minutes, until pink and opaque. Season to taste with salt.
3. Garnish with cilantro and serve immediately with lemon wedges.

SERVES 4

Gunpowder is a South Indian masala made with black gram (*urad dhaal*), dried chilies and spices. I've always loved its bold flavor and enjoy cooking prawns with South Indian spices before sprinkling the gunpowder on top at the last minute. What I adore about it is how the aromas of the spices bloom when the blend hits the hot prawns. People often laugh at the name gunpowder, assuming it's too spicy, but in reality it has a mild heat and a wonderful aroma.

Gunpowder Prawns

Gunpowder masala

2 tsp red chili flakes

2 tsp black gram (*urad dhaal*), toasted

1 tsp split chickpeas (*chana dhaal*), toasted

½ tsp cumin seeds, toasted

½ tsp sesame seeds (optional)

Salt, to taste

Gunpowder prawns

1¼ lbs large prawns, shelled and deveined

Salt, to taste

2 Tbsp vegetable oil

1 onion, finely chopped

3 cloves garlic, finely chopped

1 Tbsp finely chopped ginger

2 tomatoes, finely chopped

1-2 red bird's eye chilies

1 Tbsp Gunpowder Masala (see here), plus extra for sprinkling

¼ cup coconut milk

Cilantro, for garnish

Gunpowder masala

1 Combine all ingredients in a spice grinder or food processor and blend into a fine powder.

Gunpowder prawns

2 Lightly season prawns with salt and set aside.

3 Heat oil in a large frying pan over medium heat. Add onions and sauté for 7 minutes, until softened and translucent. Add garlic and ginger and sauté for 1–2 minutes, until fragrant.

4 Add tomatoes and chilies and cook for another 3–5 minutes, until softened. Stir in gunpowder masala and cook for 1–2 minutes, until fragrant.

5 Pour in coconut milk. Stir well and cook for another minute to allow flavors to meld.

6 Add prawns and cook for 3–5 minutes, until opaque and cooked through. (Do not overcook as they can turn rubbery.) Season to taste with salt.

7 Garnish with cilantro and a sprinkle of gunpowder masala.

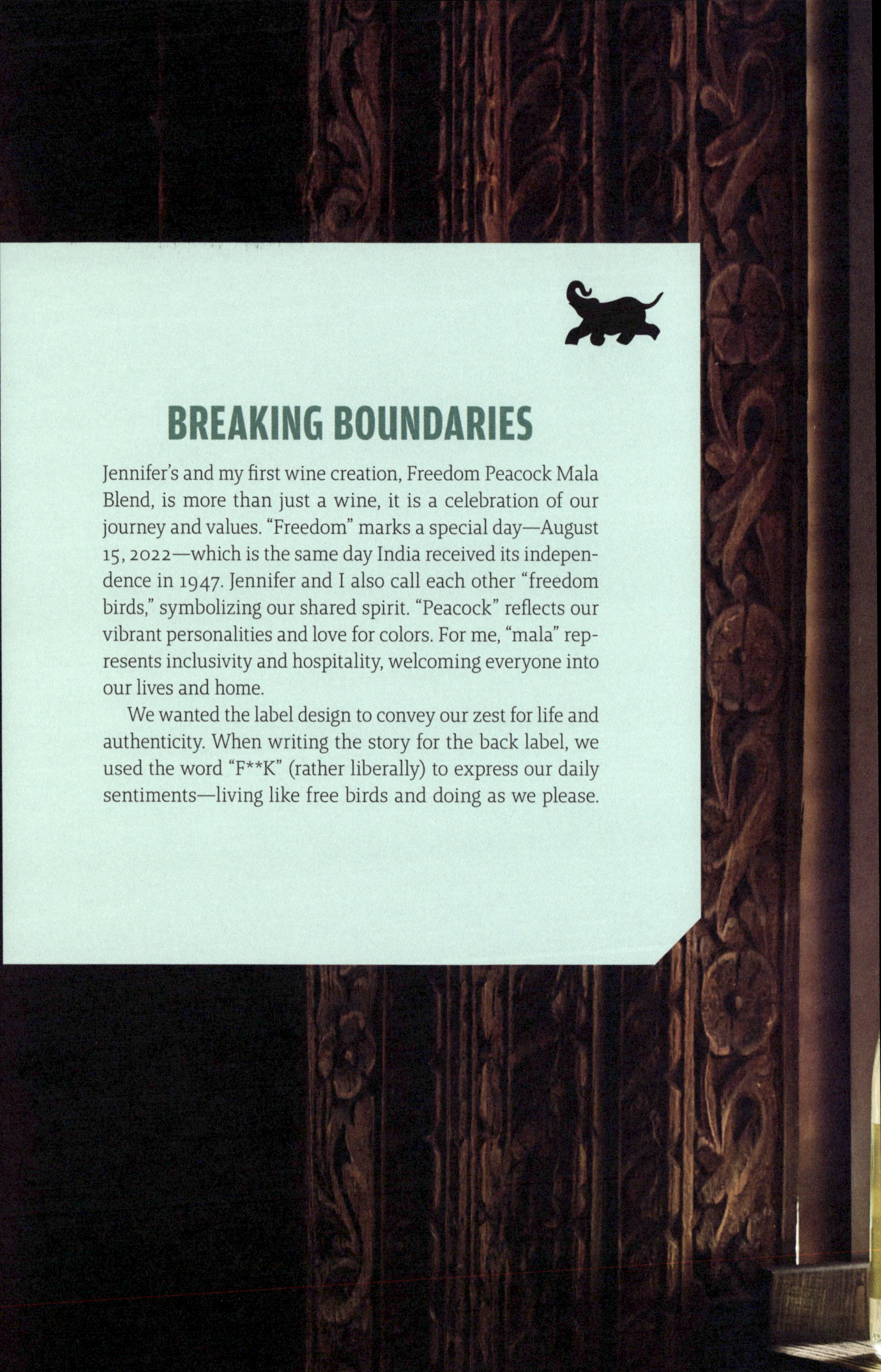

BREAKING BOUNDARIES

Jennifer's and my first wine creation, Freedom Peacock Mala Blend, is more than just a wine, it is a celebration of our journey and values. "Freedom" marks a special day—August 15, 2022—which is the same day India received its independence in 1947. Jennifer and I also call each other "freedom birds," symbolizing our shared spirit. "Peacock" reflects our vibrant personalities and love for colors. For me, "mala" represents inclusivity and hospitality, welcoming everyone into our lives and home.

We wanted the label design to convey our zest for life and authenticity. When writing the story for the back label, we used the word "F**K" (rather liberally) to express our daily sentiments—living like free birds and doing as we please.

However, when we submitted it to the BC Liquor and Cannabis Regulation Branch (LCRB) for approval, they strongly advised us to remove the profanity.

In hospitality, expressive language is part of our culture, and the playful expletive captures our true selves. Jennifer argued that no one under the age of nineteen would read it, and that everyone of legal drinking age has heard the word before. I agreed. We wrote a letter to present our view on the importance of self-expression, comparing it to uncensored musicians and artists in other fields. We made a strong case, and the liquor board conceded—we received approval! Free expression is the true meaning of life.

The label brings smiles and laughter to our patrons, but behind it and beyond the story is a great wine with crisp acidity that pairs wonderfully with our cuisine. Freedom Peacock Mala Blend is a true representation of us.

SERVES 2 (AS A MAIN COURSE) OR 4 (AS AN APPETIZER)

British Columbia mussel farms are renowned for their delicious, sustainable mussels—which explains why we chefs love them. Jaan and I love going to Granville Island and taking the Aquabus. We enjoy walking around, browsing the local shops and savoring a nice bottle of wine while indulging in BC mussels—it's the perfect way to spend the day.

In this recipe, the flavorful combination of mussels, coconut milk and spices pairs beautifully with a delicious sauvignon blanc.

Curried Mussels with Herbs

2 lbs live mussels, cleaned and debearded
2 Tbsp coconut oil
1 tsp mustard seeds
1 tsp cumin seeds
1 large onion, finely chopped
2 cloves garlic, finely chopped
1 green bird's eye chili, finely chopped (optional)
1 Tbsp grated ginger
1 tsp ground coriander
½ tsp ground turmeric
½ tsp paprika
½ cup puréed tomatoes
½ cup sauvignon blanc
½ cup coconut milk
1 cup vegetable stock
Salt and pepper, to taste
½ cup chopped cilantro
¼ cup chopped basil
¼ cup chopped dill (optional)
1 lime, cut into wedges, to serve

1. Rinse mussels thoroughly. To check if mussels are alive, tap them lightly—those that don't close should be discarded. Fresh mussels will close when tapped, indicating they're still viable and safe to cook.
2. Heat oil in a large saucepan over medium heat. Add mustard and cumin seeds and cook for 1–2 minutes, until they begin to sputter. Add onions and sauté for 5 minutes, until translucent. Add garlic, chilies (if using) and ginger. Cook for another 1–2 minutes, stirring frequently to prevent burning
3. Stir in coriander, turmeric and paprika. Cook for another 1–2 minutes to blend the spices.
4. Pour in puréed tomatoes and wine and cook for 3–4 minutes, until the sauce has slightly thickened. Pour in coconut milk and stock. Stir well and bring to a gentle simmer. Season to taste with salt and pepper.
5. Increase heat to medium-high and add mussels. Cover, then steam mussels for 5–7 minutes, until opened. Discard any mussels that are still closed. Remove from heat.
6. Add herbs and stir gently. Serve immediately with lime wedges on the side.

INFUSE LOVE INTO YOUR COOKING

Take your time and savor each step. Cooking thoughtfully, with care and attention, transforms a simple meal into something memorable. The love you invest in your food is reflected in the flavors and the joy it brings.

SERVES 2

This is a simple, flavorful way to enjoy calamari. I'm always on the lookout for great calamari, especially when I'm enjoying a cold beer on a patio. The heat and smokiness of the paprika pair perfectly with a squeeze of fresh lemon.

Spicy Paprika Calamari

- 1 lb fresh calamari, cleaned and cut into rings
- ½ cup rice flour
- 1 tsp smoked paprika
- 1 tsp pepper
- ½ tsp sweet paprika
- ½ tsp garlic powder
- ½ tsp salt
- ¼ tsp cayenne pepper (optional)
- 2 Tbsp olive oil
- 1 lemon, cut into wedges
- ¼ cup chopped parsley, for garnish

1. Pat calamari dry with a paper towel.
2. Combine calamari and flour in a bowl and toss to coat.
3. In a separate bowl, combine smoked paprika, pepper, sweet paprika, garlic powder, salt and cayenne (if using). Sprinkle the spice mixture over the calamari and toss until well coated.
4. Heat oil in a large frying pan over medium-high heat. Working in batches to avoid overcrowding, add calamari in a single layer and cook for 1–2 minutes on each side, until golden and slightly crispy. (Do not overcook as they can turn rubbery.)
5. Remove from heat. Squeeze a bit of lemon juice overtop and garnish with parsley.
6. Serve immediately with remaining lemon wedges.

THE BUTCHER'S BLOCK

At our restaurant, we are committed to serving quality, hormone-free meats from reliable suppliers. While this might make our dishes more expensive than those at many other Indian restaurants, I believe in offering food that truly honors the ingredients. At Vij's, we show gratitude to these ingredients, ensuring they are treated with the utmost respect. I enjoy grilling, pan-searing, braising and stewing the meats in our curries—marrying my French cooking techniques with my Indian heritage.

SERVES 4–6 (AS AN APPETIZER OR SNACK)

Everyone loves good chicken wings, especially when you're watching a game. Why? With its mild flavor and tender texture, chicken is the perfect canvas for a range of seasonings and cooking styles. These tandoori chicken wings are great on their own or served with a dip. In this recipe, the wings are coated in a tangy butter chicken sauce. They are delicious and messy, and designed to be eaten with your hands, so you will need to have some napkins ready.

Tandoori Chicken Wings

Tandoori chicken wings

1 cup plain yogurt
2 Tbsp tandoori masala
1 Tbsp ginger-garlic paste
1 tsp red chili powder
1 tsp ground turmeric
1 Tbsp lemon juice
Salt, to taste
2 lbs chicken wings
Whole black pepper, for garnish

Butter chicken sauce

1 cup plain yogurt
2 Tbsp lemon juice
1 tsp ground turmeric
1 tsp garam masala
1 tsp red chili powder
1 Tbsp ginger-garlic paste

Tandoori chicken wings

1. Combine all ingredients, except for chicken wings and black pepper, in a large bowl. Add chicken wings and coat in marinade. Cover and refrigerate for at least 2 hours but preferably overnight.
2. Preheat oven to 400°F (200°C). Line a baking sheet with parchment paper.
3. Place wings on the prepared baking sheet and bake for 25–30 minutes, turning halfway through.

Butter chicken sauce

4. Meanwhile, combine all ingredients in a bowl and mix well.
5. Garnish wings with black pepper, then serve hot with butter chicken sauce as a dip.

SERVES 4

This vibrant dish is a favorite of Jennifer's, and it's easy to see why. The crispy, golden chicken schnitzel is paired with a refreshing salad of sweet nectarines, tangy tomatoes and briny olives, while creamy burrata adds a luxurious finish. Panko breadcrumbs provide an extra crunch, though you can use regular breadcrumbs if you prefer.

This meal is perfect for a satisfying weeknight dinner or a special occasion, offering a balance of textures and flavors that will impress any guest. Serve it with a side of crusty bread to soak up all the delicious juices!

Chicken Schnitzel with Tomatoes, Nectarines, Olives and Burrata

Chicken schnitzel

4 chicken breasts
Salt and pepper, to taste
1 cup all-purpose flour
2 eggs, beaten
1 cup panko breadcrumbs
½ cup grated Parmesan cheese
¼ cup olive oil

Salad

2 ripe nectarines, thinly sliced
1 cup cherry tomatoes, halved
½ cup green or black olives, pitted and sliced

Assembly

1 ball burrata cheese
Chopped basil leaves, for garnish

Chicken schnitzel

1. Pound chicken breasts to a ¼-inch thickness. Season with salt and pepper.
2. To set up the breading station, place flour and eggs in separate shallow bowls. Combine breadcrumbs and Parmesan in a third bowl.
3. Dredge each chicken breast in flour, then dip into egg and coat thoroughly in the breadcrumb mixture, pressing gently to adhere.
4. Heat oil in a large skillet over medium-high heat. Add chicken and pan-fry for 3–4 minutes on each side, until golden brown and cooked through. Transfer to a paper towel-lined plate to drain.

Salad

5. In a bowl, combine all ingredients. Gently toss to mix.

Assembly

6. Arrange schnitzels on a large serving plate. Spoon salad over and around the schnitzels. Tear burrata into pieces and arrange on top. Garnish with basil. Serve immediately.

NAMASTE
VIKRAM Vij

SERVES 4–6

This vibrant, aromatic dish brings together the richness of coconut cream and the bold heat of green chilies for a truly irresistible flavor. With tender pieces of chicken simmered in a fragrant, spiced sauce, it balances warmth, earthiness and a hint of tang from the yogurt. Pair with rice or naan to soak up every last bit of the flavorful sauce.

Coconut Green Chicken

2 Tbsp vegetable oil
4–5 cloves
2–3 green cardamom pods
2 bay leaves
1 (1-inch) cinnamon stick
1 tsp cumin seeds
2 onions, finely chopped
2 Tbsp ginger-garlic paste
2 tomatoes, puréed
1 (14-oz) can coconut cream
2 tsp red chili powder
2 tsp ground coriander
1 tsp ground turmeric
4 chicken breasts, cut into bite-sized pieces
1 cup plain yogurt
Salt, to taste
1 tsp garam masala
½ cup cilantro leaves
¼ cup finely chopped green serrano chilies
½ cup mint leaves
Rice or naan, to serve

1. Heat oil in a large frying pan over medium heat. Add cloves, cardamom, bay leaves, cinnamon and cumin. Sauté for 2 minutes, until fragrant.
2. Add onions and sauté for another 2–3 minutes, until golden brown. Add ginger-garlic paste and sauté for another minute, until the raw smell disappears.
3. Add puréed tomatoes and coconut cream and simmer for 3–4 minutes, until the oil separates from the masala. Stir in chili powder, coriander and turmeric. Cook for another minute.
4. Add chicken and mix until coated in sauce.
5. Add yogurt and salt and mix well. Cover and reduce heat to low. Cook for 20–25 minutes, stirring occasionally, until chicken is cooked through. Sprinkle with garam masala and mix well. Cook for another 2–3 minutes.
6. In a blender, combine cilantro, chilies and mint and purée. Stir this mixture into the sauce. Serve hot with rice or naan.

SERVES 4

A *khadhai* is a traditional Indian wok-like pan with deep sides, perfect for stir-frying, shallow frying and simmering curries. This recipe is ideal for when you're craving a quick and spicy chicken curry—tender chicken stewed in a tomato sauce with fiery chilies. Traditionally, it's paired with scotch.

Khadhai Chicken

2 Tbsp vegetable oil
1 tsp cumin seeds
2 onions, finely chopped
2 tomatoes, puréed
1 tsp ground turmeric
1 tsp ground coriander
1 tsp ground cumin
1 tsp garam masala
1 lb boneless, skin-on chicken thighs, cut into bite-sized pieces
2 green bird's eye chilies, halved lengthwise
Salt, to taste
Cilantro leaves, for garnish
Rice or naan, to serve

1. Heat oil in a khadhai or deep frying pan over medium heat. Add cumin seeds and fry for 1 minute, until they begin to sputter.
2. Add onions and sauté for 2-3 minutes, until golden brown.
3. Add puréed tomatoes, turmeric, coriander, ground cumin and garam masala. Cook for 5-7 minutes.
4. Add chicken and cook for 20 minutes, until opaque. Stir in chilies and season to taste with salt.
5. Cover and reduce heat to low. Simmer for 20 minutes, until chicken is fully cooked and the sauce has thickened.
6. Garnish with cilantro. Serve hot with rice or naan.

SERVES 4

This dish is a true street food classic! Last year, I had an incredible roll from Khan Chacha in Delhi, a spot so iconic it draws people from all walks of life. The flavors were unforgettable, and I've since been inspired to re-create it.

The beauty of this recipe is its simplicity—it comes together quickly, especially when you use store-bought parathas, making it a perfect choice for a fast and satisfying meal.

Chicken Masala Parathas Rolls

Filling

2 Tbsp vegetable oil
1 large onion, finely chopped
2 green bird's eye chilies, finely chopped
2 tsp ginger-garlic paste
1 lb boneless, skinless chicken, cut into small pieces
2 tsp store-bought chicken masala
1 tsp ground turmeric
1 tsp red chili powder
1 tsp ground cumin
1 tsp ground coriander
Salt, to taste
1 large tomato, finely chopped
Chopped cilantro, for garnish

Assembly

4 parathas or tortillas
Green chutney
Thinly sliced onions and bell peppers
Chaat masala
Lemon wedges, to serve

Filling

1. Heat oil in a large frying pan over medium heat. Add onions and sauté for 2–3 minutes, until golden brown.
2. Stir in chilies and ginger-garlic paste and cook for another minute, until fragrant. Add chicken and cook for 20 minutes, until the meat begins to brown.
3. Mix in chicken masala, turmeric, chili powder, cumin, coriander and salt. Add chopped tomatoes and cook for another 3–4 minutes, until tomatoes are softened and the oil starts to separate from the masala. Reduce heat to medium-low, cover and simmer for 5 minutes, stirring occasionally, until fully cooked and flavors have melded.
4. Garnish with cilantro and set aside.

Assembly

5. Warm the parathas (or tortillas) in a frying pan over medium heat.
6. Spread a layer of chutney on each paratha. Spread a few tablespoons of filling down the center. Top with sliced onions and bell peppers. Sprinkle with a pinch of chaat masala. Roll the parathas tightly around the filling.
7. Serve the hot rolls with lemon wedges.

SERVES 2–3

This Goan dish has a strong Portuguese influence. Duck is a versatile meat that pairs wonderfully with spices, and in this recipe, it's combined with a fiery vindaloo sauce made from tomatoes, vinegar and a variety of spices. By the time you finish, you might need a big handkerchief to wipe the sweat off your forehead—it's that spicy! Enjoy a cold local beer to cool you down and refresh your palate.

Duck Vindaloo

2 Tbsp vegetable oil
2 onions, finely chopped
4 cloves garlic, finely chopped
2–3 green bird's eye chilies, chopped
1 Tbsp grated ginger
2 tsp ground coriander
1 tsp ground turmeric
1 tsp ground cumin
2 tomatoes, chopped
2 boneless, skinless duck breasts, cut into bite-sized pieces
1 Tbsp balsamic vinegar
Salt, to taste
1 tsp garam masala
Cilantro leaves, for garnish
Rice or naan, to serve

1. Heat oil in a frying pan over medium heat. Add onions and cook for 2–3 minutes, until golden brown. Add garlic, chilies and ginger and sauté for another 2–3 minutes, until fragrant.
2. Stir in coriander, turmeric and cumin and cook for another minute.
3. Add tomatoes and cook for 3 minutes, until tomatoes are softened and oil separates from the masala.
4. Add duck and stir to coat. Drizzle in vinegar and season with salt. Cook for 3 minutes.
5. Add enough water to cover the duck and bring to a boil. Reduce heat to medium-low and simmer for 20–25 minutes, until duck is tender and cooked through.
6. Sprinkle with garam masala and gently stir.
7. Garnish with cilantro leaves and serve hot with rice or naan.

SERVES 6

Every restaurant should have one or two signature dishes. Vij's became famous for its lamb popsicles, but I wanted another dish to rival it. I experimented with sauce and technique, adding grilled chicken to korma sauce. It became one of the more affordable options on the menu, and customers loved sharing it. In fact, I'm convinced it played a key role in helping me win the Chef of the Year award from *Vancouver Magazine* in 2015.

Vij's Chicken Korma

Chicken

1 cup plain yogurt

1 Tbsp ginger-garlic paste

Pinch of salt

2 lbs boneless, skinless chicken thighs

Korma sauce

2 Tbsp vegetable oil

1 large onion, finely chopped

2 cloves garlic, finely chopped

1 Tbsp grated ginger

2 Tbsp store-bought korma paste

1 tsp ground cumin

1 tsp ground coriander

1 tsp ground turmeric

1 tsp red chili powder

1 cup coconut milk

½ cup heavy cream

¼ cup ground almonds

Assembly

Salt and pepper, to taste

Chopped cilantro, for garnish

Chopped walnuts, for garnish

Rice or naan, to serve

Chicken

1. In a bowl, combine yogurt, ginger-garlic paste and salt. Add chicken and mix to coat. Cover, then refrigerate for at least 1 hour, or overnight for best results.
2. Preheat a grill or grill pan over medium-high heat. Remove chicken from the marinade, then place it on the grill. Grill for 5–7 minutes on each side, until fully cooked. Set aside to rest for 1–2 minutes, then cut into bite-sized pieces.

Korma sauce

3. Heat oil in a Dutch oven over medium heat. Add onions and sauté for 10–15 minutes, until golden brown and caramelized. Add garlic and ginger and cook for another 2–3 minutes, until fragrant.
4. Stir in korma paste, cumin, coriander, turmeric and chili powder. Cook for 2–3 minutes until fragrant.
5. Stir in coconut milk and cream. Add ground almonds, then gently simmer for 10 minutes, allowing sauce to thicken.

Assembly

6. Add chicken to the pan, stirring to coat with the sauce. Season to taste with salt and pepper. Simmer for another 5–10 minutes to allow flavors to meld.
7. Garnish with cilantro and walnuts. Serve hot with rice or naan.

SERVES 4–6 (AS AN APPETIZER OR SIDE DISH)

This recipe is a tribute to my aunt, who used to make it for me all the time in Amritsar. Cold meat with bones is rare and not often prepared, but once you taste it, you'll be hooked on the rich flavors. I love serving pickled goat with warm parathas alongside.

Pickled Goat

1 cup mustard oil
1 tsp fenugreek seeds
1 tsp fennel seeds
1 tsp nigella seeds
2 lbs bone-in goat meat, cut into pieces
2 Tbsp red chili powder
1 Tbsp ground turmeric
Salt, to taste
1 cup white vinegar
Parathas, to serve

1. Heat oil in a frying pan over medium heat until it starts to smoke. Reduce heat to low. Add fenugreek, fennel and nigella seeds.
2. Add goat and cook for 30–45 minutes, until fully browned on all sides. Mix in chili powder, turmeric and salt.
3. Pour in vinegar, then increase heat to medium-low. Simmer for 1–2 hours, until the meat is tender and the liquid has reduced by half. Set aside to cool, then chill in the fridge.
4. Serve cold with parathas.

SERVES 6

Growing up, meat was a rare treat, enjoyed only once a week. Despite my constant requests for more, my mother believed in the benefits of moderation, so our diet was predominantly vegetarian, with a variety of dhaals and fresh vegetables.

My eating habits shifted when I moved to Austria in the 1990s, where European culinary traditions encouraged me to incorporate meat into my daily meals. My first challenge was preparing beef tongue—quite a departure from the plant-based diet I had known. To become a well-rounded chef, I had to broaden my palate, and over time I grew to appreciate a variety of meats. *Dum gosht*, with its rich and hearty flavors, quickly became a favorite for special occasions.

Slow, Slow, Very Slow Cooked Goat

- 3 Tbsp vegetable oil or ghee
- 2 onions, finely chopped
- 2 Tbsp ginger-garlic paste
- 4 tomatoes, finely chopped
- 2¼ lbs bone-in goat meat, cut into pieces
- 1 cup plain yogurt
- 2 tsp ground coriander
- 1 tsp ground cumin
- 1 tsp garam masala
- ½–1 tsp red chili powder
- ½ tsp ground turmeric
- Salt, to taste
- Cilantro leaves, for garnish
- Rice, naan or roti, to serve

1. Heat oil (or ghee) in a Dutch oven over medium heat. Add onions and sauté for 2–3 minutes, until golden brown.
2. Add ginger-garlic paste and sauté for another 2–3 minutes, until fragrant. Add tomatoes and cook for 3–4 minutes, until tomatoes are softened and the oil starts to separate from the masala.
3. Add goat meat and mix well. Cook for 5–7 minutes, stirring occasionally, until the meat is lightly browned on all sides.
4. In a bowl, combine yogurt, coriander, cumin, garam masala, chili powder, turmeric and salt. Pour the mixture into the pan and mix well to coat the meat. Cover and reduce heat to low. Cook for 2–3 hours, stirring occasionally, until the meat is tender enough to fall off the bone. If needed, add a little water to prevent the goat from sticking to the bottom of the pan and to maintain the desired gravy-like consistency of the sauce.
5. Season to taste with salt and spices.
6. Garnish with cilantro. Serve hot with rice, naan or roti.

SERVES 4 (AS AN APPETIZER)

Pork is not commonly eaten throughout India, but it has a cherished spot in South Indian cuisine, with dishes like pork vindaloo and jasmine rice being favorites. This recipe uses pork tenderloin, which can be either grilled or oven-cooked, making it an ideal appetizer when paired with homemade pickles or chutneys.

Spice-Encrusted Pork Tenderloin

Pork tenderloin

1 Tbsp ground coriander
1 Tbsp ground cumin
1 Tbsp paprika
1 tsp ground turmeric
1 tsp salt
1 tsp pepper
2 Tbsp olive oil
1 (1-lb) pork tenderloin
Chutney (page 63) or pickles, to serve

Rice

2 cups jasmine rice
1 Tbsp olive oil or butter
2 cloves garlic, finely chopped
2½ cups chicken or vegetable stock
Juice of 1 lemon, plus extra to taste
Salt, to taste

Pork tenderloin

1. Preheat oven to 375°F (190°C) or preheat a grill over medium-high heat.
2. In a small bowl, combine coriander, cumin, paprika, turmeric, salt and pepper.
3. Brush oil over the pork, then evenly coat it in the spice blend. Place tenderloin on a baking sheet (or the grill). Roast for 25–30 minutes, until the internal temperature reaches 145°F (63°C). (Alternatively, if grilling, cook for 20 minutes, turning occasionally.)

Rice

4. Meanwhile, rinse rice under cold running water until water runs clear. This removes excess starch and yields fluffy rice.
5. Heat oil (or butter) in a medium saucepan over medium heat. Add garlic and sauté for 1–2 minutes, until fragrant and golden.
6. Stir in rice to coat. Cook for 1–2 minutes to deepen the flavor.
7. Pour in stock and lemon juice. Add a pinch of salt. Stir briefly, then bring to a boil. Reduce heat to low, cover and simmer for 15 minutes, until rice is cooked and liquid has been absorbed. Remove from heat and set aside, covered, for 5 minutes.

To serve

8. Set pork tenderloin aside to rest for 5 minutes.
9. Fluff up rice with a fork. Season to taste with lemon juice or salt.
10. Slice tenderloin (it should be pink and medium-cooked). Transfer to a serving plate and serve with rice and homemade pickles or chutneys.

FROM AWE TO ACCLAIM

I had long admired Chef Thomas Keller and dreamed of visiting The French Laundry. After years of running Vij's, I finally saved enough to experience this culinary landmark.

With close friends, I booked a private room and requested in advance that Chef Thomas Keller prepare our meal. We spared no expense, indulging in exquisite wines and dishes, including a smoked salmon tartare in an ice cream cone. Despite cooking with many world-renowned chefs, it was the most flawless meal I'd ever had.

Afterward, I went to thank Chef Thomas Keller in person. I introduced myself as a young chef from Vancouver with an Indian restaurant called Vij's and handed him my card. His brief response—"Okay"—left a lasting impression, but I understood that I was just another young chef in a long line of admirers.

Years later, on December 10, 2016, my phone rang. To my surprise, it was Chef Thomas Keller, calling from California. He was hosting a prestigious fundraiser at Caesars Palace and invited me to prepare my signature lamb popsicles for the event. I didn't mention our earlier encounter and accepted the invitation.

I found myself alongside culinary giants like Ming Tsai, Curtis Stone and Paul Bocuse's son Jérôme. Nervously, I

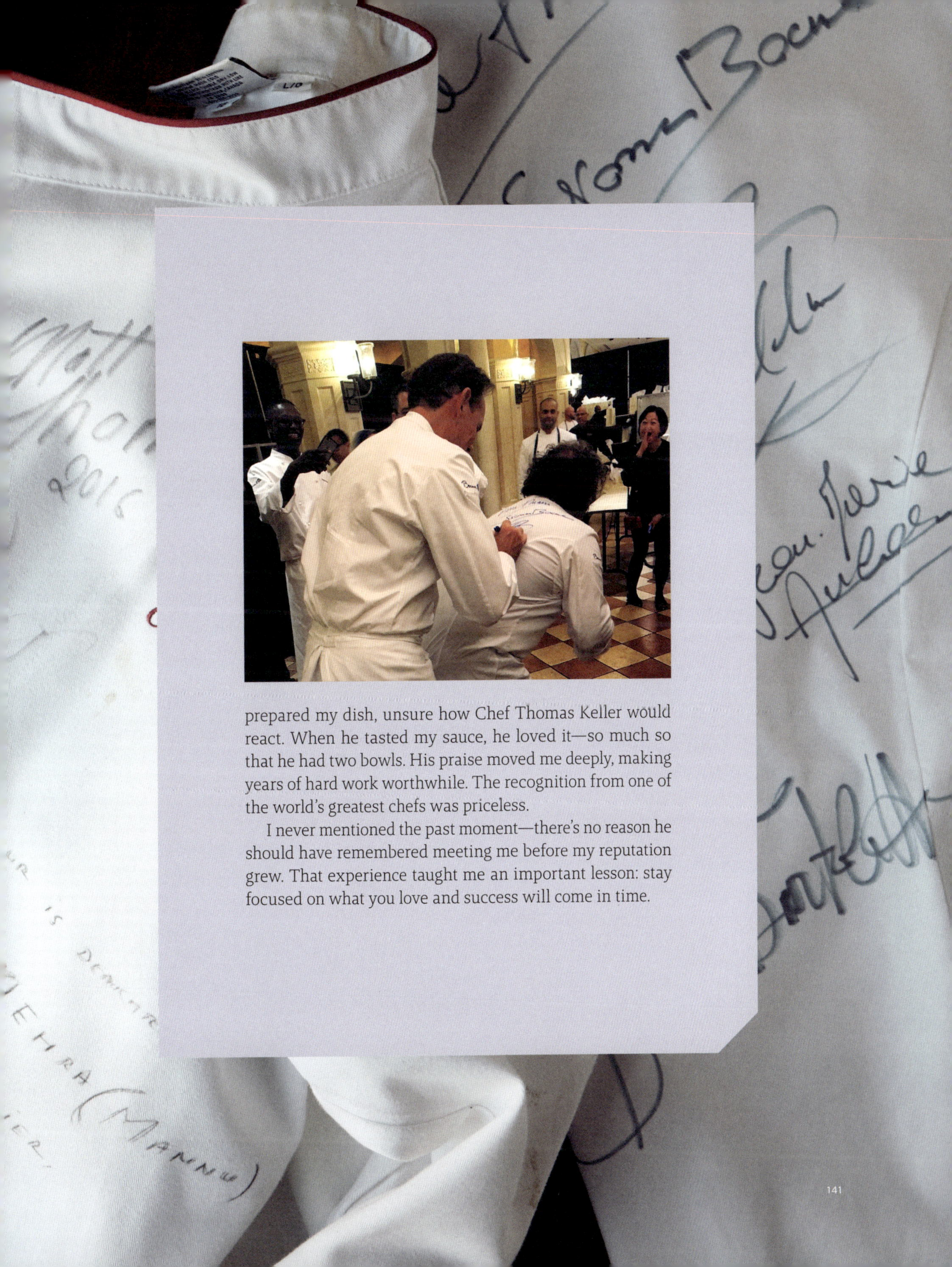

prepared my dish, unsure how Chef Thomas Keller would react. When he tasted my sauce, he loved it—so much so that he had two bowls. His praise moved me deeply, making years of hard work worthwhile. The recognition from one of the world's greatest chefs was priceless.

I never mentioned the past moment—there's no reason he should have remembered meeting me before my reputation grew. That experience taught me an important lesson: stay focused on what you love and success will come in time.

SERVES 4

Wild boar has a flavor similar to pork, so my goal was to create a delicious, spicy sausage—like chorizo or currywurst—without the casing. A final sear adds a nice char, which pairs beautifully with sweet date-tamarind or cilantro-mint chutney. Wild boar, a sustainable meat option, is usually available at specialty stores and can also be substituted with pork.

Wild Boar (or Pork) Kebabs

- 1 lb ground wild boar or pork
- 1 onion, finely chopped
- 2 cloves garlic, finely chopped
- 2 green bird's eye chilies, finely chopped
- 2 Tbsp chopped cilantro
- ½ Tbsp grated ginger
- 1 tsp ground cumin
- 1 tsp ground coriander
- ½ tsp ground turmeric
- ½ tsp garam masala
- Salt, to taste
- Vegetable oil, for grilling
- Sweet chutney, such as date-tamarind or cilantro-mint, to serve

1. Combine all sausage ingredients in a bowl and mix well. Use your hands to form the mixture into kebabs, about 4–5 inches long and 1 inch thick.
2. Heat oil on a grill pan or in a frying pan over medium heat. Add kebabs and cook for 5–7 minutes on each side, until browned and cooked through.
3. Serve with a sweet chutney.

SERVES 4

My daughters loved this mild dish when they were young and would always help me by breading the pork loins. The potatoes are simply flavored with butter and parsley—easy, yet so delicious. You could pair the schnitzel with a flavored mayonnaise too; I personally enjoy Sriracha mayo for a bit of heat.

Pork Schnitzel with Parsley Potatoes

Potatoes

1 lb baby potatoes
2 Tbsp butter
¼ cup chopped parsley
Salt and pepper, to taste

Schnitzel

4 thin pork loins
Salt and pepper, to taste
1 cup all-purpose flour
2 eggs, beaten
1 cup breadcrumbs
2 Tbsp vegetable oil
Flavored mayo, to serve

Potatoes

1. Bring a saucepan of water to a boil. Add potatoes and cook for 20–25 minutes, until tender. Drain, then toss with butter and parsley. Season with salt and pepper.

Schnitzel

2. Season pork with salt and pepper.
3. Set up flour, eggs and breadcrumbs in separate bowls. Dredge each pork loin in flour, then dip it in egg and coat in breadcrumbs.
4. Heat oil in a frying pan over medium heat. Add pork and cook for 3–4 minutes on each side, until golden brown and cooked through. Transfer to a paper towel–lined plate to drain.
5. Serve the schnitzel with parsley potatoes and your favorite flavored mayo.

SERVES 6

When I first opened Vij's, Chef Michael Allemeier would visit every Saturday afternoon. We'd make this delicious soup together on a small electric stove, talking about our lives and career challenges. It was a rare chance to connect, as we hadn't spent much time together when we worked at Bishop's. Three decades later, we re-created this soup at a dinner at the Fairmont Jasper Park Lodge, surrounded by friends who had supported us over the years. There was laughter, warmth and a deep sense of camaraderie.

This classic Indian soup combines fragrant coconut milk, tender leftover chicken and a perfect blend of spices. More than just a dish, it's a celebration of friendship and shared memories.

Mulligatawny Soup

1 Tbsp vegetable oil
1 onion, finely chopped
2 cloves garlic, finely chopped
1 Tbsp grated ginger
1 carrot, chopped
1 apple, peeled and chopped
1 Tbsp curry powder
1 tsp ground cumin
1 tsp ground coriander
1 tsp ground turmeric
1 tsp red chili powder
1 cup red lentils, rinsed
4 cups chicken stock
2 cups cooked shredded chicken
1 (14-oz) can coconut milk
Salt and pepper, to taste
Chopped cilantro, for garnish
Rice or naan, to serve

1 Heat oil in a large saucepan over medium heat. Add onions, garlic and ginger and sauté for 5–7 minutes, until onions are translucent.

2 Stir in carrots and apples and sauté for 3–5 minutes, until they start to soften. Stir in curry powder, cumin, coriander, turmeric and chili powder. Cook for another minute, until fragrant.

3 Stir in lentils, coating them in the spices. Pour in stock and bring to a boil. Reduce heat to medium-low and simmer for 20–25 minutes, until lentils are tender.

4 Add chicken and coconut milk and stir well to combine. Season to taste with salt and pepper. Simmer for another 10 minutes to allow flavors to meld.

5 To serve, ladle soup into bowls. Garnish with cilantro and serve hot with rice or naan.

A SINGLE BITE, A LIFE TRANSFORMED

This cherished recipe marks the beginning of my journey in Canada. Every time I mention goulash, it fills me with joy and brings tears to my eyes.

While working at a well-known ski resort in Austria, I met a gentleman originally from Central Europe who was a regular at the restaurant. He loved spicy food, so the maître d' asked me to prepare something with a bit of heat, given my Indian background.

My mom had sent me cumin seeds and her homemade garam masala—which I treasured, since Austrian food felt bland to me. I sautéed onions with the spices, added them to the goulash, and served it with homemade bread.

Soon after, I was called into the dining room. I feared the patron might be upset by the spice level. At that time, it was common to tease chefs—especially an Indian chef in a mostly white kitchen. I was often ridiculed for my background, with comments like "You're the best East Indian

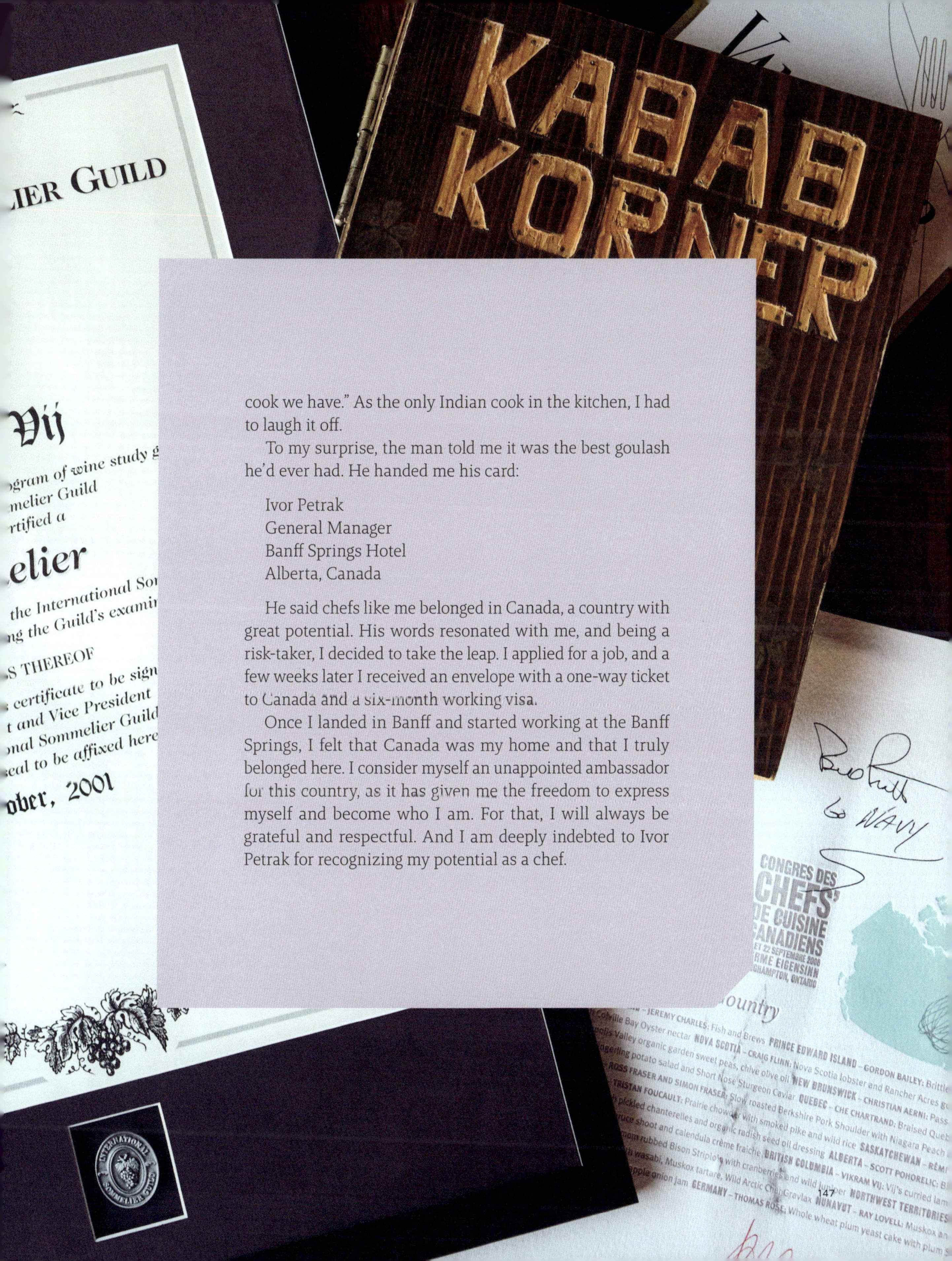

cook we have." As the only Indian cook in the kitchen, I had to laugh it off.

To my surprise, the man told me it was the best goulash he'd ever had. He handed me his card:

Ivor Petrak
General Manager
Banff Springs Hotel
Alberta, Canada

He said chefs like me belonged in Canada, a country with great potential. His words resonated with me, and being a risk-taker, I decided to take the leap. I applied for a job, and a few weeks later I received an envelope with a one-way ticket to Canada and a six-month working visa.

Once I landed in Banff and started working at the Banff Springs, I felt that Canada was my home and that I truly belonged here. I consider myself an unappointed ambassador for this country, as it has given me the freedom to express myself and become who I am. For that, I will always be grateful and respectful. And I am deeply indebted to Ivor Petrak for recognizing my potential as a chef.

SERVES 6

This hearty goulash combines the rich flavors of traditional Central European goulash with a unique twist of Indian spices. Tender stewing beef, vegetables and a savory broth are infused with the warmth of sweet paprika, along with the bold and aromatic notes of cumin, garam masala and caraway seeds. A perfect balance of earthy and spicy flavors, this soup is the comforting and flavorful dish that brought me to Canada (page 146).

Ivor Petrak's Goulash

- 2 Tbsp olive oil
- 1 large onion, finely chopped
- 1 tsp cumin seeds
- 3 cloves garlic, finely chopped
- 1 lb stewing beef, cut into bite-sized pieces
- 1 tsp salt
- ½ tsp pepper
- 2 Tbsp Hungarian sweet paprika
- 1 Tbsp tomato paste
- 4 cups beef stock
- 2 carrots, sliced
- 1 large potato, diced
- 1 green bell pepper, seeded, deveined and diced
- 1 large tomato, diced
- 1 tsp caraway seeds
- 1 tsp dried marjoram
- 1 tsp garam masala
- 1 bay leaf
- ¼ cup chopped parsley or cilantro, for garnish
- Crusty bread or dumplings, to serve

1. Heat oil in a large saucepan over medium heat. Add onions and sauté for 2–3 minutes, until softened and golden.
2. Add cumin seeds, increase heat to medium-high and sauté for 2 minutes. Add garlic and sauté for another minute. Add beef, salt and pepper, and brown for 5–7 minutes on all sides.
3. Stir in paprika and tomato paste and cook for 1 minute to release the flavors. Pour in stock and 2 cups of water.
4. Add carrots, potatoes, bell peppers and tomatoes. Stir in caraway seeds, marjoram, garam masala and the bay leaf.
5. Bring to a boil, then reduce heat to low. Cover and simmer for 1½–2 hours, stirring occasionally, until beef is tender and flavors are well-developed.
6. Season to taste with more salt, pepper and/or paprika. Discard bay leaf.
7. Ladle the hot goulash into serving bowls, garnish with parsley (or cilantro) and serve with crusty bread or dumplings.

SERVES 4

This mild yet flavorful stew from Jennifer was one of her mama's favorite dishes. I love it during the colder months, as it warms and comforts the body. I recommend pairing this curry with homemade naan for a truly satisfying meal.

Beef Curry

Beef
2 tomatoes, chopped
2 scallions, chopped
2 cloves garlic, chopped
1 onion, chopped
1 Tbsp curry powder
1 Tbsp white wine vinegar
Salt, to taste
1 lb stewing beef, cut into 1-inch cubes

Curry sauce
1 Tbsp curry powder
1–2 cloves garlic, finely chopped

Assembly
1 Tbsp vegetable oil
Rice or naan, to serve

EMBRACE IMPERFECTION
Not every dish needs to be flawless. Sometimes the most delicious meals are the ones that are a bit rustic, made with genuine effort and authenticity. Don't be afraid to let your food show its character.

Beef
1. Combine all ingredients, except for beef, in a large bowl. Add beef and rub the mixture into the meat. Set aside for 10–15 minutes.

Curry sauce
2. Combine curry powder and garlic in a small bowl. Add 1 cup of water to form a medium-thin sauce.

Assembly
3. Heat oil in a frying pan over medium heat. Add curry sauce and stir for 1–2 minutes, until it begins to simmer.
4. Add the beef mixture. Bring to a boil, then cover and reduce heat to medium-low.
5. Simmer for 15–20 minutes, stirring often to prevent sticking, until beef is browned. Add 1 cup of water and simmer for another 25 minutes, until beef is tender and fully cooked. The sauce should be thick but not completely reduced—add more water if needed.
6. Serve hot with rice or naan.

LAUGHS, LESSONS AND LASTING MEMORIES

When chef and documentarian Anthony Bourdain came to Vancouver, he chose to feature three restaurants on his show *No Reservations*: Cioppino's, Tojo's and Vij's. I was already familiar with Tony's work as the executive chef at the now defunct Les Halles and due to his book *Kitchen Confidential*, which I've read twice. Everything he wrote in it still rings true.

We filmed part of our segment at an Indian market. I showed him the spices and explained how important it is for a Punjabi market to have signs in both Punjabi and English and to be recognized internationally. At the time, the market vendors and shoppers were asking to take my photo, which was ironic because Tony was the internationally acclaimed celebrity! When he asked why no one was asking him for pictures, I replied, "Dude, this is my town." We laughed and had a great shoot.

Years later, Tony and I met up at a pub in New York. This time, everyone came up to Tony while I was ignored. We laughed about it that evening, sitting under a lamppost, drinking and talking about life. That was the last time I saw him. Tony brought the culinary world to the forefront with his writings and his shows.

I am still saddened by the loss of this dear friend. I miss you, Tony.

SERVES 4–6

Venison is very lean and requires a degree of time to prepare because the blood needs to be drained from the meat. I like to put it into a colander set over a bowl and leave it to drain overnight. (Otherwise, the venison tastes too gamey.) This family favorite recipe is not for the faint of heart!

Venison Biryani

- 2 lbs venison, cubed
- 2 cups basmati rice
- 2 Tbsp vegetable oil or ghee
- 2 large onions, thinly sliced
- 1 cup plain yogurt
- 2 Tbsp biryani masala
- 2 tsp ground turmeric (divided)
- Salt, to taste
- 1 cup beet juice
- Cilantro, for garnish
- Mint, for garnish

1. Rinse venison under cold running water. Soak it in water for at least 1 hour to remove the blood, replenishing the water several times.
2. Soak rice in water for 30 minutes. Drain.
3. Heat oil (or ghee) in a large saucepan over medium heat. Add onions and sauté for 2–3 minutes, until golden brown.
4. Add venison, yogurt, biryani masala, 1 teaspoon of turmeric and salt. Cook for 3 minutes, until the venison is lightly browned on all sides and the spices are well mixed. Cover, reduce heat to low and cook for another 20–25 minutes, until venison is tender. (There should be enough liquid released, but if the meat starts to stick to the pan, add ½ to 1 cup of water.)
5. Combine 1 cup of drained rice, 2 cups of water and the remaining teaspoon of turmeric in one pot, and combine the other cup of drained rice, 1 cup of water and the beet juice in a separate pot. Bring both pots to a boil, stir, then reduce heat to low. Cover and cook for 20 minutes, until the rice is tender.
6. Layer the venison biryani in a serving dish, starting with the venison and its sauce. Top with a layer of beet rice and a layer of turmeric rice. Garnish with cilantro and mint and serve.

THE GLOW OF NOSTALGIA

When I bought my first restaurant in 1994, originally called Café Arabia, the sale came with vibrant Moroccan lamps. They were colorful, funky and kitschy—adding charm to the small space. And as I was a one-man show back then (doing all the cooking, serving and cleaning myself), I believed the lamps reflected the café and myself perfectly.

When the restaurant became too busy for the space, we moved to a larger location. Designer Marc Bricault, a regular at Vij's, offered to design new lamps for the space. At the same time, one of my other regulars, named Gregory, was opening a hair salon. It desperately needed some decor items, but he was on a tight budget and in a bind. To help out, I sold him my beloved lanterns for a steal at $500 and they looked stunning in the salon, their new home.

Twenty years later, I had all but forgotten about the lamps. I had heard that Gregory was struggling after losing his

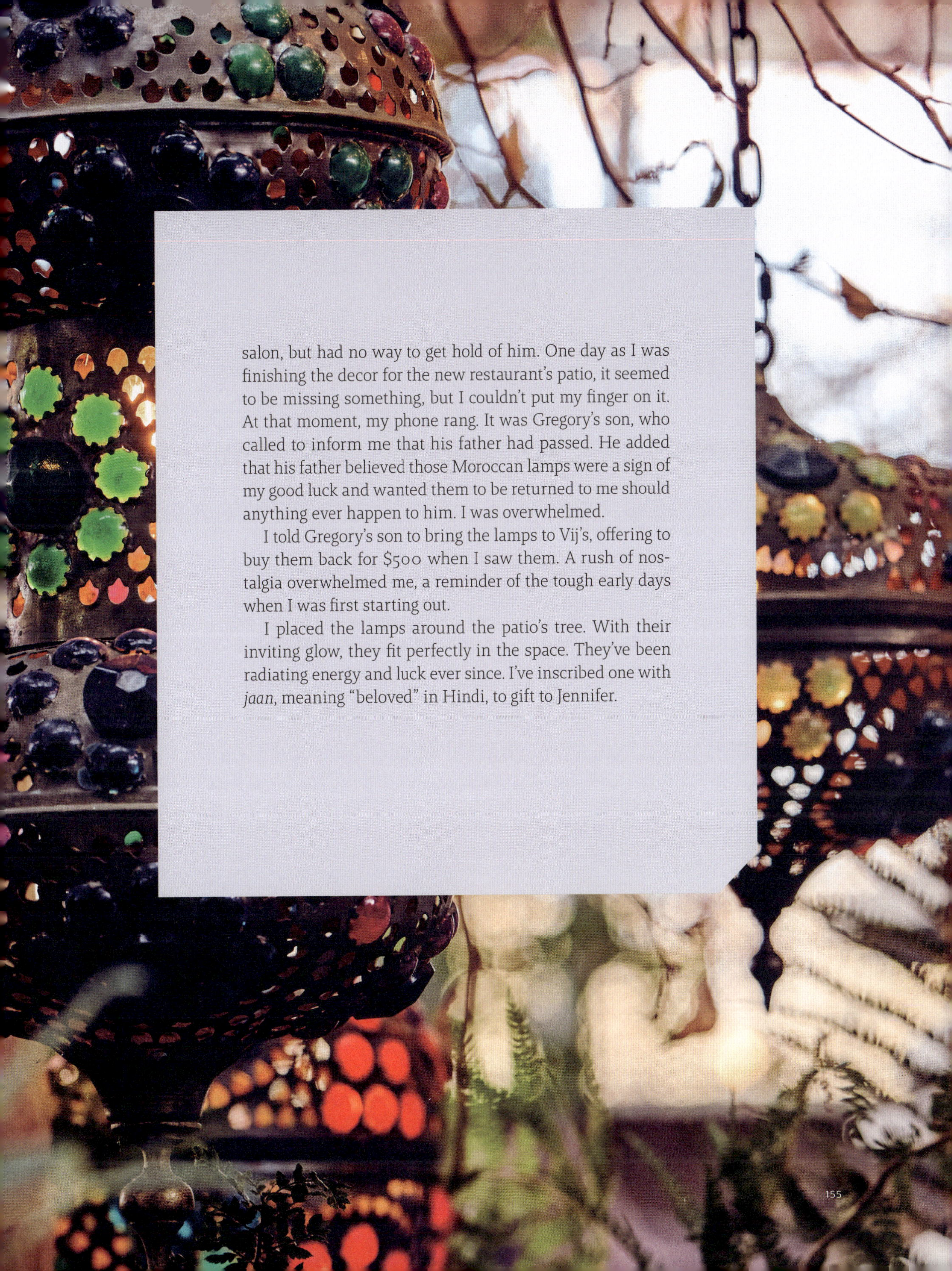

salon, but had no way to get hold of him. One day as I was finishing the decor for the new restaurant's patio, it seemed to be missing something, but I couldn't put my finger on it. At that moment, my phone rang. It was Gregory's son, who called to inform me that his father had passed. He added that his father believed those Moroccan lamps were a sign of my good luck and wanted them to be returned to me should anything ever happen to him. I was overwhelmed.

I told Gregory's son to bring the lamps to Vij's, offering to buy them back for $500 when I saw them. A rush of nostalgia overwhelmed me, a reminder of the tough early days when I was first starting out.

I placed the lamps around the patio's tree. With their inviting glow, they fit perfectly in the space. They've been radiating energy and luck ever since. I've inscribed one with *jaan*, meaning "beloved" in Hindi, to gift to Jennifer.

SERVES 4

This recipe is one of my favorites to make for my daughters, especially when paired with a fresh tomato and feta salad. I use ground goat meat and a bold mix of spices, with pepper and red chili flakes from India being the standout flavors that really make this dish pop. It's the perfect meal to keep your teenagers coming back home for more—I'm convinced there's something about the rich, warming spices that draws them in!

My Spaghetti Bolognese

2 Tbsp olive oil
1 large onion, finely chopped
4 cloves garlic, finely chopped
1 lb ground goat meat
1 carrot, finely chopped
2 cups tomato purée
1 tsp red chili flakes
1 tsp pepper
1 tsp ground cumin
Salt, to taste

To serve
Cooked spaghetti
Basil, for garnish
Grated Parmesan

1. Heat oil in a large frying pan over medium heat. Add onions and garlic and sauté for 3 minutes, until golden brown.
2. Add goat and cook for 25 minutes, until fully browned.
3. Add carrots, tomato purée, chili flakes, pepper, cumin and salt, then add 1 cup of water. Stir well.
4. Reduce heat to medium-low, cover and simmer for 45 minutes, stirring occasionally.
5. Serve sauce over cooked spaghetti. Garnish with basil and sprinkle with Parmesan.

SERVES 4

This rich, aromatic dish is served throughout India. The smooth sauce is made with yogurt in the north and coconut milk in the south. You can skip the cashews and almonds if preferred, but they add a lovely creaminess.

Lamb Korma

- 2 Tbsp vegetable oil or ghee
- 2 onions, finely chopped
- 2 Tbsp ginger-garlic paste
- 1 green bird's eye chili, halved lengthwise (optional)
- 2 tomatoes, finely chopped
- ¼ cup unsalted cashews, soaked in water for 30 minutes
- ¼ cup ground almonds
- 1 lb boneless leg of lamb, cut into bite-sized pieces
- 1 tsp ground coriander
- 1 tsp red chili powder
- 1 tsp garam masala
- ½ tsp ground cumin
- ½ tsp ground turmeric
- ½ cup plain yogurt
- Salt, to taste
- Cilantro leaves, for garnish
- Rice, naan or roti, to serve

1. Heat oil (or ghee) in a Dutch oven over medium heat. Add onions and sauté for 2–3 minutes, until golden brown.
2. Add ginger-garlic paste and chili (if using) and sauté for another 2–3 minutes, until fragrant.
3. Add tomatoes and cook for 2 minutes, until tomatoes are softened and the oil separates from the masala.
4. Meanwhile, drain the cashews. In a blender, combine cashews and ground almonds. Blend to a smooth paste, adding a little water if needed.
5. Once tomatoes are mostly broken down, add lamb to the pan. Mix well and cook for 5–7 minutes, until lamb is browned on all sides.
6. Add coriander, chili powder, garam masala, cumin and turmeric. Stir to coat lamb in spices.
7. Stir in yogurt and cook for another 3–4 minutes, until it is incorporated into the sauce. Add the cashew-almond paste and stir again. The sauce should have the consistency of a thin gravy. If needed, add water.
8. Bring to a gentle simmer. Cover, reduce heat to low and cook for 30–40 minutes, until lamb is tender and cooked through. Stir occasionally to prevent the korma from sticking to the bottom. Season to taste with salt and spices.
9. Garnish with cilantro and serve hot with rice, naan or roti.

SERVES 4

The name *rogan josh* comes from *rogan*, meaning "intense red color," and *josh*, meaning "strong" or "passionate." My first experience with this dish was in Rajasthan, one sweltering, dusty day. Seeking refuge at a roadside eatery, I was greeted by irresistible aromas, and I ordered lamb rogan josh with tandoori roti and pickled red onions.

When my meal arrived, I eagerly took a bite—only to unknowingly chew on a Kashmiri chili. The fiery heat burned my mouth, and I found myself wiping sweat from my forehead with my shirt. Despite the spice, the dish was so delicious I couldn't stop eating. By the end of the meal, my shirt was drenched, and my nose was running, but the tender lamb and rich sauce left an unforgettable impression.

Years later, while studying at the Salzburger Hotelfachschule in Austria, I prepared a goulash stew that reminded me of lamb rogan josh—though with a milder paprika flavor. To balance the heat, serve this aromatic dish with plain yogurt on the side.

Chili-Spiced Lamb Rogan Josh

3 Tbsp vegetable oil or ghee
4–5 cloves
4–5 green cardamom pods
2–3 bay leaves
2 cinnamon sticks
1 tsp cumin seeds
2 onions, finely chopped
2 Tbsp ginger-garlic paste
1 green bird's eye chili, finely chopped (optional)
4 tomatoes, finely chopped
1 tsp ground coriander
1 tsp ground cumin
1 tsp ground paprika
1 tsp Kashmiri chili powder
½ tsp ground turmeric
Salt, to taste
1 lb leg of lamb, cut into bite-sized pieces
Cilantro leaves, for garnish
Rice, naan or roti, to serve

1 Heat oil (or ghee) in a Dutch oven over medium heat. Add cloves, cardamom, bay leaves, cinnamon and cumin seeds. Sauté for 1 minute, until fragrant. Add onions and sauté for 2–3 minutes, until golden brown.

2 Add ginger-garlic paste and chilies (if using) and sauté for another 2–3 minutes, until the raw smell disappears.

3 Add tomatoes and cook for another 3–4 minutes, until tomatoes are softened and the oil starts to separate from the masala.

4 Add coriander, cumin, paprika, chili powder, turmeric and salt and stir well.

5 Add lamb and mix well. Cook for 5–7 minutes, until the lamb is browned on all sides.

6 Pour in 1 cup of water and stir to incorporate. Cover and reduce heat to low. Cook for 45–60 minutes, stirring occasionally, until lamb is tender and cooked through. If needed, add more water to prevent the lamb rogan josh from sticking to the bottom. Season to taste with salt and spices.

7 Garnish with cilantro. Serve hot with rice, naan or roti.

SERVES 4

During the colder winter months, my grandmother and mother would always prepare this warm, comforting classic from my hometown of Amritsar, filling the house with its inviting aromas. Even now, whenever I make this dish, I'm instantly transported back to those cherished times.

Lamb pairs beautifully with spinach, and this dish makes a perfect showstopper for serving a group. Enjoy it with pickled ginger, pickles and naan or chapati.

Spinach Lamb

Bunch of spinach, well rinsed
2 Tbsp vegetable oil
1 tsp cumin seeds
2 onions, finely chopped
1 Tbsp ginger-garlic paste
2 tomatoes, chopped
1 lb leg of lamb, cubed
1 tsp ground coriander
1 tsp garam masala
Salt, to taste
Naan, to serve

1. Bring a saucepan of water to a boil. Add spinach and cook for 1 minute. Drain, then transfer to a bowl of ice water. Put spinach into a blender and purée until smooth.
2. Heat oil in a frying pan. Add cumin seeds and fry for 1 minute, until they begin to sputter.
3. Add onions and ginger-garlic paste and sauté for 2–3 minutes, until onions are golden brown. Add tomatoes and cook for 2–3 minutes, until softened.
4. Add lamb and cook for 20 minutes, until lamb is tender and cooked through. Stir in puréed spinach, coriander, garam masala and salt. Simmer for 3–4 minutes, to allow the flavors to meld.
5. Serve hot with naan.

SWEET ENDINGS

I love Indian desserts, especially the flavors of nuts, rose petals and aromatic spices. I try not to indulge too often, though, as I typically get my sugar fix from wine. In the afternoons, when I arrive at the restaurant, the kitchen crew and I have chai time. We review the lists, sip chai and enjoy some Indian sweets. I always indulge, and it's a great opportunity to hear the cooks' stories before the dinner rush begins.

SERVES 4

I had panna cotta for the first time when I visited Italy. Its velvety texture and subtle sweetness paired perfectly with fruit, creating a luxuriously indulgent dessert that reminds me of Indian custard.

For this global twist on a classic, I combine traditional Italian panna cotta with a tropical element—it's one of my favorite ways to end a meal.

Mango Panna Cotta

- 2½ tsp gelatin powder
- 1 cup heavy cream
- ½ cup milk
- ¼ cup sugar
- 1 cup fresh or canned mango purée
- 1 tsp vanilla extract
- Mint leaves, for garnish

1. Sprinkle gelatin over 2 tablespoons of water in a small bowl. Set aside for 5 minutes to bloom.
2. In a saucepan, combine cream, milk and sugar. Warm over medium heat, stirring until sugar has dissolved. Do not bring to a boil. Remove from heat.
3. Stir in the bloomed gelatin until fully dissolved. Mix in mango purée and vanilla extract.
4. Pour mixture into serving glasses or molds and refrigerate for at least 4 hours, until set.
5. Garnish with mint, then serve.

SERVES 4

Traditional rice pudding, or kheer, can sometimes feel a bit plain. In this version, I've combined my French culinary training with Indian techniques to create a simple yet elegant dessert. The addition of cardamom and the aromatic touch of rose petals gives it a fragrant twist that elevates this classic. It's a delightful dish that's perfect for larger gatherings when you need to double or triple the recipe, and it offers a beautiful balance of creaminess and spice that's both comforting and unique.

Kheer with Rose Petals

1 cup basmati rice
4 cups milk
1 cup sugar
1 tsp ground cardamom
¼ cup chopped almonds and pistachios, plus extra for garnish
1 tsp fresh edible rose petals, for garnish

1. Rinse rice thoroughly under cold running water until the water runs clear. Soak rice in a bowl of water for 20–30 minutes. Drain.
2. Bring milk to a boil in a heavy-bottomed pan. Reduce heat to low, then add rice. Simmer for 25–30 minutes, until rice is fully cooked and milk has thickened and is reduced by half. Stir occasionally to prevent the pudding from sticking to the bottom of the pan.
3. Stir in sugar until dissolved. Mix in cardamom and nuts and simmer for another 5–10 minutes, until thick and sticky.
4. Remove from heat, garnish with more nuts and set aside to cool slightly.
5. The rice pudding can be served warm or chilled. If serving chilled, refrigerate for a few hours. Garnish with fresh rose petals before serving.

MAKES 48 COOKIES

Jennifer's chocolate chip cookies are the perfect balance of chewy and crispy, with a rich, buttery flavor and just the right amount of sweetness. I make them when I need a quick treat to bring to a house party or when friends come over. They're the best fresh out of the oven.

Chocolate Chip Cookies

- 1 cup (2 sticks) salted butter, softened
- 1 cup sugar
- 1 cup packed light brown sugar
- 2 tsp vanilla extract
- 2 eggs
- 3 cups all-purpose flour
- 1 tsp baking soda
- ½ tsp baking powder
- 1 tsp sea salt
- 2 cups chocolate chips

ENGAGE YOUR SENSE OF SMELL

Pause for a moment to inhale the aroma of your meal, whether it's the fresh scent of herbs and spices or the comforting smell of food as it bakes—this simple act can amplify your connection to the dish and build anticipation.

1. Preheat oven to 350°F (180°C). Line 2 baking sheets with parchment paper.
2. In a large bowl, cream together butter and sugars until light and fluffy. Beat in vanilla extract and eggs, one at a time, until fully incorporated.
3. In a separate bowl, whisk together flour, baking soda, baking powder and sea salt. Gradually add the dry ingredients to the wet and mix until just combined.
4. Fold in chocolate chips.
5. Using a cookie scoop or two tablespoons, drop dough onto the prepared baking sheets, spacing cookies 2 inches apart.
6. Bake for 10–12 minutes, until the edges are golden brown, but the centers are still slightly soft.
7. Set aside to cool on the baking sheets for 3–5 minutes. Transfer to a wire rack to cool completely.

SERVES 4

This delightful twist on a classic Indian pudding replaces rice with nutrient-dense chia seeds, which are packed with omega-3 fatty acids, fiber and protein. With its creamy, custard-like texture, natural sweetness courtesy of the almond milk and vibrant burst of berries, it's a triumphant guilt-free dessert that satisfies sweet cravings while nourishing the body. And one more thing: it is ridiculously quick and easy to put together.

Chia Seed Kheer with Berries

¼ cup chia seeds

1 cup almond milk or milk of your choice

¼ cup honey or maple syrup

½ tsp ground cardamom

1 cup mixed berries, such as blueberries, strawberries and raspberries

Mint leaves, for garnish

1. In a bowl, combine chia seeds, milk, honey (or maple syrup) and cardamom. Set aside for 15 minutes, stirring occasionally, until thickened.
2. Divide the chia pudding into individual serving bowls and top with mixed berries.
3. Garnish with mint leaves and serve chilled.

VEGETARIAN

SERVES 6–8

I love serving this kulfi alongside Jennifer's freshly baked Chocolate Chip Cookies (page 167) for the perfect East-meets-West dessert combo. Kulfi is a rich, creamy frozen Indian treat made from simmered milk and infused with aromatic spices like cardamom and saffron—it's an indulgent dessert that practically melts in your mouth.

I prepare this dessert using traditional kulfi molds, but popsicle molds or small cups work just as well if you don't have the classic ones on hand.

Pistachio Cardamom Kulfi

4 cups milk
1 cup condensed milk
½ cup heavy cream
½ cup sugar
½ tsp ground cardamom
10–15 strands saffron (optional)
½ cup pistachios, finely chopped (divided)
¼ cup almonds, finely chopped (divided)
1 tsp rose water (optional)

1. Bring milk to a boil in a heavy-bottomed saucepan over medium heat, stirring frequently to prevent it from sticking.
2. Reduce heat to low and simmer for 45 minutes, stirring occasionally, until the milk has reduced by half.
3. Stir in condensed milk, cream and sugar and mix until sugar has fully dissolved.
4. Add cardamom, saffron (if using) and half of the pistachios and almonds. Simmer for another 15–20 minutes, stirring frequently. Set aside to cool slightly.
5. Stir in rose water (if using) for an extra layer of flavor.
6. Pour mixture into small serving cups. Garnish with the remaining chopped pistachios and almonds and cover with plastic wrap. Freeze for at least 6–8 hours, until completely set.
7. Remove from the freezer, then set aside at room temperature for a few minutes to slightly soften. Serve with dessert spoons.

VEGETARIAN

SERVES 6

I have vivid memories of sipping chai on railway station platforms and then breaking the disposable clay cups on the ground—a ritual that's as much a part of the experience as the drink itself. Those handcrafted chai cups now adorn the ceiling of our lounge at Vij's.

When I first opened the restaurant, I wanted every guest to feel at home, so I served chai and snacks as a warm welcome. At the time, this was a bit of a novelty in the restaurant world, where food and labor costs were always a concern. Inevitably, there would be leftover chai, so I decided to create chai kulfi—a delightful way to marry the rich, spiced flavors of traditional Indian chai with the creamy texture of kulfi. It's become the perfect way to end a meal, both comforting and unique.

Chai Kulfi

2 cups milk
1 cup condensed milk
1 cup heavy cream
2 chai tea bags or 2 Tbsp loose chai tea
4–5 cloves
3–4 green cardamom pods, lightly crushed
1 cinnamon stick
1 (½-inch) piece ginger, sliced
¼ tsp ground nutmeg
¼ tsp pepper
¼ cup chopped nuts, such as almonds, pistachios and cashews (optional)
Saffron, for garnish (optional)

1. In a saucepan, combine milk, condensed milk and cream. Bring the mixture to a gentle simmer over medium heat, stirring occasionally.
2. Add chai, cloves, cardamom, cinnamon, ginger, nutmeg and pepper. Stir to combine, then simmer gently for 10–15 minutes. Stir occasionally to infuse the flavors. Strain through a fine-mesh sieve.
3. Stir in nuts (if using). Pour the mixture into small serving cups and cover with plastic wrap. Place in the freezer and freeze for at least 6 hours but preferably overnight, until the kulfi sets completely.
4. Remove from the freezer, then set aside at room temperature for a few minutes to slightly soften.
5. Garnish the chai kulfi with saffron strands (if using), for a touch of flavor and elegance, and serve with dessert spoons.

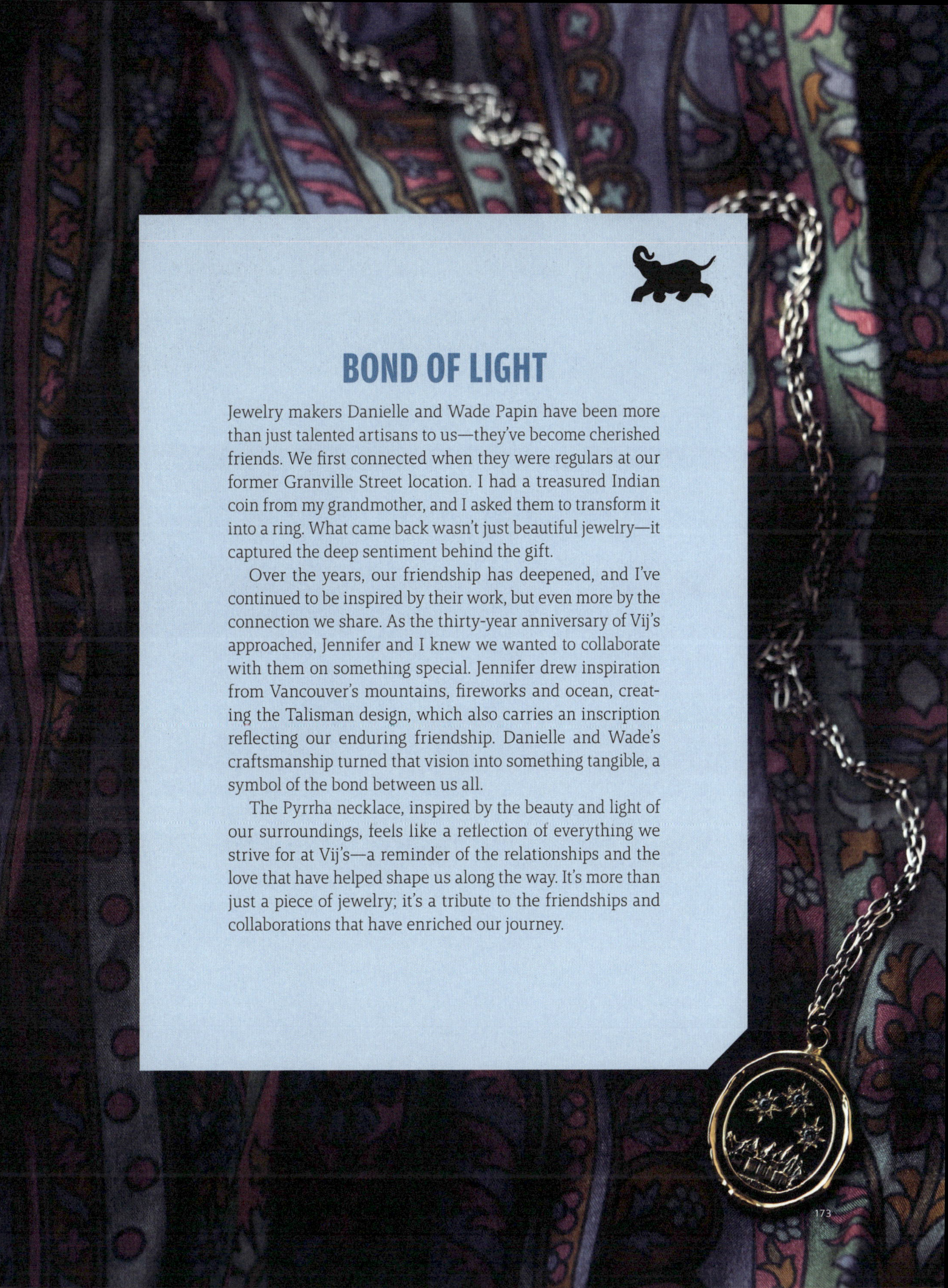

BOND OF LIGHT

Jewelry makers Danielle and Wade Papin have been more than just talented artisans to us—they've become cherished friends. We first connected when they were regulars at our former Granville Street location. I had a treasured Indian coin from my grandmother, and I asked them to transform it into a ring. What came back wasn't just beautiful jewelry—it captured the deep sentiment behind the gift.

Over the years, our friendship has deepened, and I've continued to be inspired by their work, but even more by the connection we share. As the thirty-year anniversary of Vij's approached, Jennifer and I knew we wanted to collaborate with them on something special. Jennifer drew inspiration from Vancouver's mountains, fireworks and ocean, creating the Talisman design, which also carries an inscription reflecting our enduring friendship. Danielle and Wade's craftsmanship turned that vision into something tangible, a symbol of the bond between us all.

The Pyrrha necklace, inspired by the beauty and light of our surroundings, feels like a reflection of everything we strive for at Vij's—a reminder of the relationships and the love that have helped shape us along the way. It's more than just a piece of jewelry; it's a tribute to the friendships and collaborations that have enriched our journey.

VEGETARIAN

SERVES 4

This creamy, refreshing ice cream captures the delicate fragrance of rose petals, transforming a simple treat into something extraordinary. With its hint of floral elegance, this ice cream is a unique and indulgent dessert that's both sophisticated and easy to make at home. Perfect for impressing guests or adding a touch of luxury to any occasion!

Rose Water Ice Cream

- 2 cups heavy cream
- 1 cup milk
- ¾ cup sugar (divided)
- 5 egg yolks
- 1 Tbsp rose water, plus extra to taste
- ¼ tsp vanilla extract (optional)
- 2 drops pink food coloring (optional)
- 1 tsp fresh edible rose petals, for garnish (optional)

EXPERIENCE THE TEMPERATURE OF YOUR FOOD

Consider the warmth of a hearty dish or the coolness of a refreshing salad. The temperature of food adds complexity to both flavor and texture, enriching the sensory experience of eating.

1. In a saucepan, combine cream, milk and half of the sugar. Heat over medium heat, stirring occasionally, until the mixture is hot but not boiling.
2. In a separate bowl, whisk together egg yolks and the remaining sugar until smooth and slightly thickened. Slowly pour a ladle of the hot cream mixture into the egg yolks while whisking continuously to temper the eggs. Gradually add 1–2 more ladles of the hot cream.
3. Pour the egg mixture back into the saucepan with the remaining cream and cook over low heat, stirring constantly, until the mixture thickens enough to coat the back of a spoon (at about 170°F/77°C).
4. Remove from heat, then stir in rose water and vanilla extract (if using). Add pink food coloring, if desired.
5. Pour custard through a fine-mesh sieve into a clean bowl to remove any cooked egg. Cover and refrigerate for at least 4 hours, or overnight, until chilled.
6. Pour the chilled custard into an ice cream maker and churn according to the manufacturer's instructions until the ice cream reaches a soft-serve consistency.
7. Transfer to a lidded container and freeze for at least 2 hours, until firm.
8. Scoop into bowls and garnish with fresh rose petals (if using).

VEGETARIAN

SERVES 8–10

Though I had never considered myself a dessert chef, everything changed in the winter of 2023 when I received a beautiful mixer from someone I love deeply. I cherished it, and began baking more from that day forward. In December 2023, I baked my first cheesecake ever to share at Vij's with my team, and this has become my go-to recipe ever since. The sweetness of peach purée combined with the creamy richness of cheesecake makes this dessert feel both indulgent and refreshing.

Just Peachy Cheesecake

2 cups graham cracker crumbs
½ cup (1 stick) butter, melted
3 (8-oz) packages cream cheese, softened
1 cup sugar
1 tsp vanilla extract
3 eggs
1 cup fresh or canned peach purée
1 cup sliced peaches, for topping

1. Preheat oven to 325°F (160°C).
2. In a medium bowl, combine graham cracker crumbs and butter and mix until combined. Press the mixture into a 9-inch springform pan, in an even layer.
3. Bake for 10 minutes, then set aside to cool.
4. Meanwhile, in a large bowl, combine cream cheese, sugar and vanilla extract and mix until smooth and creamy. Add eggs, one at a time, beating well after each addition. Stir in peach purée until well combined.
5. Pour the cream cheese batter into the springform pan. Bake for 55–60 minutes, until center is set.
6. Turn off the oven, open the door slightly and leave the cheesecake to cool for 1 hour.
7. Refrigerate the cheesecake for at least 4 hours, but preferably overnight.
8. Top with sliced peaches and serve.

VEGETARIAN

SERVES 8–10

Who doesn't love fudge? I'm hooked on this delicious treat and I love surprising guests with a homemade batch! What makes this version special is the addition of cardamom and saffron, giving the fudge a unique twist. I promise it will be a standout at any table.

I typically source my condensed milk from a local farm, but store-bought works just as well.

Indian Fudge

¼ cup ghee, plus extra for greasing
2 cups milk powder
1 (14-oz) can condensed milk
½ tsp ground cardamom
Pinch of saffron strands (optional)
Chopped almonds or pistachios, for garnish

1. Grease a 6- × 10-inch pan with ghee.
2. Heat ghee in a non-stick saucepan over medium heat. Whisk in milk powder and stir continuously to avoid lumps.
3. Stir in condensed milk and cook for 3–4 minutes, until it thickens slightly.
4. Add cardamom and saffron (if using). Pour into the prepared pan. Garnish with chopped nuts.
5. Set aside for 40 minutes to cool completely, then refrigerate for 1 hour to chill.
6. Cut fudge into portions and serve.

SERVES 8–10

Cuisines are like rivers—they should flow freely, without boundaries. In a traditional tiramisu, coffee flavors the ladyfingers. Here, we use rich, spiced Indian chai to infuse the dessert with a unique, flavorful twist.

Purists might find it hard to digest, but when it comes to cooking, intuition leads the way, sparking new ideas and creations. This is one of those dishes.

Indian Tiramisu

Masala chai syrup

- 4 green cardamom pods, lightly crushed
- 2 cloves
- 1 small cinnamon stick
- 1 star anise
- 1 (½-inch) piece ginger, sliced
- 2 Tbsp black tea leaves, such as English breakfast
- ½ cup sugar

Flavored mascarpone

- 1 cup mascarpone cheese
- 1 cup heavy cream
- ½ cup icing sugar
- 1 tsp vanilla extract

Assembly

- 24 ladyfinger biscuits
- ¼ cup cocoa powder, for dusting
- ½ cup finely chopped pistachios or almonds (optional)

Masala chai syrup

1. Bring 2 cups of water to a boil in a saucepan. Add all ingredients, except for sugar, and simmer for 5 minutes. Stir in sugar until dissolved and simmer for another 5 minutes. Strain syrup, then set aside to cool completely.

Flavored mascarpone

2. Combine all ingredients in a large mixing bowl. Whisk together until smooth and creamy. Set aside.

Assembly

3. Dip a ladyfinger into the cooled syrup. (Do not soak it, just a quick dip to absorb some flavor.) Place it in a 6- × 12-inch dish (or use individual serving glasses). Repeat with more ladyfingers until the bottom of the dish is fully covered. Spread a layer of the mascarpone mixture on top, using about half of it.
4. Repeat with another layer of ladyfingers and mascarpone.
5. Cover and refrigerate for at least 4 hours, preferably overnight, to allow flavors to meld.
6. To serve, top the tiramisu with a dusting of cocoa powder. Garnish with pistachios or almonds (if using).

MAKES 12

Prepare this labor-intensive dessert when you really want to impress at the dinner table. While these sweet samosas take time and patience to make, the indulgent blend of dark chocolate, cinnamon and a hint of chili makes every bit worth the effort. The contrast of crispy, golden wrappers with a rich, spiced ganache filling is a surprising and delightful twist on a traditional favorite, perfect for anyone looking to level up their dessert game.

Chocolate Samosas with Spiced Ganache

Chocolate filling

¼ cup heavy cream
½ cup chopped dark chocolate
2 Tbsp sugar
¼ tsp ground cinnamon
¼ tsp red chili powder (optional)

Assembly

2 cups vegetable oil, for deep-frying
12 samosa wrappers
1 egg, for egg wash
Icing sugar, for dusting

Chocolate filling

1. Heat cream in a small saucepan over medium heat until it starts to simmer.
2. Place chocolate in a bowl, then pour in cream. Set aside for 1 minute. Stir until smooth.
3. Stir in sugar, cinnamon and chili powder (if using). Season to taste with more chili powder, if you like! Set aside to cool slightly, until the chocolate filling is thick and spreadable. If desired, you can refrigerate it briefly to firm up.

Assembly

4. Pour oil into a deep fryer or deep saucepan and heat to a temperature of 350°F (177°C).
5. Lay out a samosa wrapper. Place a small spoonful of the chocolate filling at one corner of the wrapper. Fold that end of the wrapper into a triangle, enclosing the filling. Continue the folding process until the entire wrapper is folded up. Brush a little egg wash along the edges to seal. Repeat with the remaining wrappers and filling.
6. Working in batches, carefully lower the samosas into the hot oil, taking care not to splash it. Deep-fry for 2–3 minutes on each side, until golden. Using a slotted spoon, transfer the samosas to a paper towel-lined plate to drain. Set aside to cool slightly.
7. Dust with icing sugar and serve warm.

Metric Conversion Chart

Volume

Imperial or US	Metric
⅛ tsp	0.5 mL
¼ tsp	1 mL
½ tsp	2.5 mL
¾ tsp	4 mL
1 tsp	5 mL
½ Tbsp	8 mL
1 Tbsp	15 mL
1½ Tbsp	23 mL
2 Tbsp	30 mL
¼ cup	60 mL
⅓ cup	80 mL
½ cup	125 mL
⅔ cup	165 mL
¾ cup	185 mL
1 cup	250 mL
1¼ cups	310 mL
1⅓ cups	330 mL
1½ cups	375 mL
1⅔ cups	415 mL
1¾ cups	435 mL
2 cups	500 mL
2¼ cups	560 mL
2⅓ cups	580 mL
2½ cups	625 mL
2¾ cups	690 mL
3 cups	750 mL
4 cups/1 quart	1 L
5 cups	1.25 L
6 cups	1.5 L
7 cups	1.75 L
8 cups	2 L
12 cups	3 L

Liquid measures (for alcohol)

Imperial or US	Metric
½ fl oz	15 mL
1 fl oz	30 mL
2 fl oz	60 mL
3 fl oz	90 mL
4 fl oz	120 mL

Cans and jars

Imperial or US	Metric
6 oz	170 g
14 oz	398 mL
19 oz	540 mL
28 oz	796 mL

Weight

Imperial or US	Metric
½ oz	15 g
1 oz	30 g
2 oz	60 g
3 oz	85 g
4 oz (¼ lb)	115 g
5 oz	140 g
6 oz	170 g
7 oz	200 g
8 oz (½ lb)	225 g
9 oz	255 g
10 oz	285 g
11 oz	310 g
12 oz (¾ lb)	340 g
13 oz	370 g
14 oz	400 g
15 oz	425 g
16 oz (1 lb)	450 g
1¼ lbs	570 g
1½ lbs	675 g
2 lbs	900 g
3 lbs	1.4 kg
4 lbs	1.8 kg
5 lbs	2.3 kg
6 lbs	2.7 kg

Linear

Imperial or US	Metric
⅛ inch	3 mm
¼ inch	6 mm
½ inch	12 mm
¾ inch	2 cm
1 inch	2.5 cm
1¼ inches	3 cm
1½ inches	3.5 cm
1¾ inches	4.5 cm
2 inches	5 cm
2½ inches	6.5 cm
3 inches	7.5 cm
4 inches	10 cm
5 inches	12.5 cm
6 inches	15 cm
7 inches	18 cm
10 inches	25 cm
12 inches (1 foot)	30 cm
13 inches	33 cm
16 inches	41 cm
18 inches	46 cm
24 inches (2 feet)	60 cm
28 inches	70 cm
30 inches	75 cm
6 feet	1.8 m

Temperature (For oven temperatures, see chart in next column)

Imperial or US	Metric
90°F	32°C
120°F	49°C
125°F	52°C
130°F	54°C
140°F	60°C
150°F	66°C
155°F	68°C
160°F	71°C
165°F	74°C
170°F	77°C
175°F	80°C
180°F	82°C
190°F	88°C
200°F	93°C
240°F	116°C
250°F	121°C
300°F	149°C
325°F	163°C
350°F	177°C
360°F	182°C
375°F	191°C

Oven temperature

Imperial or US	Metric
200°F	95°C
250°F	120°C
275°F	135°C
300°F	150°C
325°F	160°C
350°F	180°C
375°F	190°C
400°F	200°C
425°F	220°C
450°F	230°C
500°F	260°C
550°F	290°C

Baking pans

Imperial or US	Metric
5- × 9-inch loaf pan	2 L loaf pan
9- × 13-inch cake pan	4 L cake pan
11- × 17-inch baking sheet	30 × 45 cm baking sheet

Acknowledgments

A heartfelt tribute to my fellow chefs and restaurant owners: your perseverance and dedication in the challenging world of food and beverage are nothing short of inspiring. Your passion shines through, even in the face of adversity, and your hard work is a testament to your unwavering commitment to quality and creativity. Whether your restaurants have stood the test of time or have had to close their doors, your contributions are deeply respected and appreciated.

I'd like to extend a special thank you to my mentor John Bishop, who made the difficult decision to close his restaurant. I have learned invaluable lessons from you, and I am forever grateful for your guidance. You will always hold a special place.

Thank you to all my guests over the years who've made Vij's Restaurant what it is today. It would not be here without you.

To Jennifer: your creativity and expertise have been a constant source of inspiration, helping me develop this cookbook—and with it convey our passion, respect and love for what we can do together.

And to my daughters, Nanaki and Shanik: thank you for reminding me to dream big.

Index

Page numbers in italics refer to photos.

About the Authors

Chef Vikram Vij is a celebrated culinary icon known for revolutionizing Indian cuisine in Canada through his acclaimed restaurant, Vij's, and has received numerous accolades, including the prestigious Chef of the Year award from *Vancouver Magazine* (2015). Renowned for his innovative approach that fuses traditional Indian flavors with local ingredients, Vikram's culinary artistry has earned him a following and critical acclaim, including a spot on *Top Chef Canada*. Beyond his restaurant, he is an author and a prominent television personality, inspiring home cooks with his engaging presence. With a commitment to elevating Indian cuisine and promoting diversity in the culinary world, Vikram continues to be a beacon of excellence and creativity in the gastronomic landscape. He is based in Vancouver.

Jennifer Muttoo is a dedicated champion of the hospitality industry, bringing extensive expertise in hotel and restaurant management to every project. As the leader of J Marketing, she specializes in elevating the social media presence of restaurants and emerging chefs, while celebrating the artistry and innovation behind memorable dining experiences for renowned brands like Vij's Restaurant. Beyond her marketing role, she holds the position of director of food and beverage at a hotel. With more than two decades of experience and an unwavering passion for the industry, Jennifer's multifaceted approach blends culinary excellence, storytelling, event coordination, design aesthetics and strategic hospitality management.

www.vijs.ca

Vijsrestaurant

Recipes are chef-tested.

25 26 27 28 29 5 4 3 2 1

Cataloguing data is available from Library and Archives Canada
ISBN 978-1-77327-261-0 (hbk.)

Design by Jessica Sullivan | DSGN Dept.
Photography by Gabriel Cabrera
Food and prop styling by Bri Beaudoin

Editing by Michelle Meade
Copy editing by Pam Robertson
Proofreading by Breanne MacDonald
Indexing by Iva Cheung

Printed and bound in China by Shenzhen Reliance Printing Co., Ltd.

Figure 1 Publishing Inc.
Vancouver BC Canada
www.figure1publishing.com